Robert Frost &
THE NEW ENGLAND RENAISSANCE

Robert Frost

& THE NEW ENGLAND RENAISSANCE

GEORGE MONTEIRO

THE UNIVERSITY PRESS OF KENTUCKY

Scholarly publisher for the Commonwealth,
serving Bellarmine College, Berea College, Centre
College of Kentucky, Eastern Kentucky University,
The Filson Club, Georgetown College, Kentucky
Historical Society, Kentucky State University,
Morehead State University, Murray State University,
Northern Kentucky University, Transylvania University,
University of Kentucky, University of Louisville,
and Western Kentucky University.

Editorial and Sales Offices: Lexington, Kentucky 40506-0336

Library of Congress Cataloging-in-Publication Data

Monteiro, George.
　　Robert Frost and the New England renaissance / George Monteiro.
　　　　p.　cm.
　　Bibliography: p.
　　Includes index.
　　ISBN 0-8131-1649-X
　　1. Frost, Robert, 1874-1963—Criticism and interpretation.
　　2. Frost, Robert, 1874-1963—Sources.　3. American literature—New
England—History and criticism.　4. American literature—19th
century—History and criticism.　5. New England—Intellectual life.
I. Title.
PS3511.R94Z793　1988
811'.52—dc19　　　　　　　　　　　　　　　　　　88-5479

To STEVE, EMILY, and KATE

CONTENTS

Preface: Raking the Leaves Away   ix

1. Directives   1

PART ONE. Dickinson, Etc.

2. Dangling Conversation   9
3. One Hand Clapping   24
4. Designs   34
5. Roads and Paths   44

PART TWO. The Thorosian Poem

6. Education by Metaphor   57
7. Bonfires   66
8. Economy   76
9. Smoke   82
10. Solitary Singer   90
11. Swinging   99

PART THREE. Mainly Emerson

12. Nature's Gold   115
13. Linked Analogies   123
14. Dominion   130
15. Substantiation   138

PART FOUR. Coda

16. Tributaries   147

Notes   153
Index   171

Raking the Leaves Away

What you say isn't yours. A poet can only brag about form.
—Robert Frost (1930s)

ROBERT FROST's critics tend to ignore the important fact that he was not for the most part brought up on the farms of New England. Surprisingly, he lived in San Francisco until he was eleven and then in Lawrence, Massachusetts, throughout his years in grammar school and high school. Indeed, not until the early days of his marriage to Elinor White, his high school sweetheart, did the poet whose name would in time evoke rural New England (particularly New Hampshire and Vermont) turn to farming for his livelihood.

Whether or not Frost chose to be a farmer primarily because he expected farming to provide him with poetic images, metaphors, and subject matter cannot be ascertained. But he did sometimes act as if his only interest lay in following Emerson's advice.

The first care of a man settling in the country should be to open the face of the earth to himself by a little knowledge of Nature, or a great deal, if he can; of birds, plants, rocks, astronomy; in short, the art of taking a walk. This will draw the sting out of frost, dreariness out of November and March, and the drowsiness out of August. . . . But the uses of the woods are many, and some of them for the scholar high and peremptory. When his task requires the wiping out from memory

"all trivial fond records
That youth and observation copied there,"
["*Hamlet*, I, 5"]

he must leave the house, the streets and the club, and go to wooded uplands, to the clearing and the brook. Well for him if he can say with the old minstrel, "I know where to find a new song."[1]

Yet inasmuch as Frost began learning about rural matters rather late in life for such education (and he extolled the virtues of being "versed in country things"), he found himself with considerable catching up to do.

Not the least of his tasks was to discover as much as possible as fast as possible about the fauna and flora of northern New England. His friend Carl Burrell taught him about the flowers and the birds (as well as the stars), but the poet could not know everything all at once, and naturally he made mistakes. He imagined, for example, that "geese roost in the trees even in winter" and said as much, to the consternation of the readers of a poultry trade journal.[2] On another occasion he published a poem, "The Quest of the Orchis," only to discover years later that the flower he had found was really the gentian, not the elusive orchis.[3] It is no wonder that as late as 1930 Frost confessed, only half-jokingly, to his "masquerade as a Vermonter."[4]

The importance of Frost's early displays of ignorance of simple natural facts should not be overstated, but such instances certainly demonstrate that New England's preeminent pastoral poet was not born to the rural manner. The facts and details of his assiduous search for knowledge in his early adulthood are laid out in the first volume of Lawrance Thompson's biography.[5] John Kemp's study traces many of the implications of those facts for Frost's decisions regarding his poetry and his public image. Kemp notes that Frost tried his hand at several different kinds of verse before assuming his identity as a farmer-poet with the publication in 1913 of A Boy's Will, his first volume.[6]

In his quest for knowledge the young Frost had recourse to books ranging from Emerson's essays and Thoreau's Walden to Mrs. William Starr Dana's How to Know the Wild Flowers. It became increasingly important to him to read Emerson, Thoreau, and Emily Dickinson, in particular, and occasionally also Henry Wadsworth Longfellow or William James, as he sought to establish his public image. The poems and essays of these writers offered an abundance of material that Frost incorporated into his New England poetry. Judging by his practice, we can see that Frost accepted Emerson's observations, at least implicitly: "Our debt to tradition through reading and conversation is so massive, our protest or private addition so rare and insignificant

. . . that, in a large sense, one would say there is no pure orig-
inality. All minds quote. Old and new make the warp and woof
of every moment. There is no thread that is not a twist of these
two strands."[7] We see the logic thus of following Frost's in-
sistence that "a poem is best read in the light of all the other
poems ever written."[8] Aimed at the reader who would achieve
poetic literacy, this dictum applies particularly to readers of
Frost's own poetry. Many of his most valuable poems can be best
approached within contexts provided by the poems and essays
of his New England precursors.

That, in sum, is the basic idea of this book. It links the
various chapters, which might otherwise be viewed as discrete
essays. In their aggregate, moreover, these pieces sustain a crit-
ical method that is both contextual and historically literary.

In the years since I began to think about the advantages of
considering Robert Frost's poetry within a New England literary
context, I have been influenced by the work of many scholars.
My mention of some of them in the notes to this book barely
hints at my appreciation of that influence.

Other debts have been more direct. I am grateful for the
instruction and encouragement given me by teachers of poetry
whose teaching carried well beyond the time spent in the class-
room, particularly Sharon Brown, Daniel Hoffman, and Hyatt
Waggoner.

I wish also to acknowledge with gratitude the friendship and
learned counsel of David Hirsch, who, along with Barton St.
Armand, for longer than any of us cares to remember, has dis-
cussed literature with me in the Ivy Room and elsewhere. Along
the way I have enjoyed the privilege of learning from other
friends, particularly the late William Hester, Louis Leiter, Mario
D'Avanzo, Sandra Baker, and Leonard Quirino. To them I can
only say, belatedly, thank you. I am grateful, too, to Brenda
Murphy, whose reading of the manuscript was most helpful.

My thanks to Candida Hutter, who deftly and expertly kept
me supplied with clean copies of the manuscript.

I wrote and published portions of this book before I began to
think about making it a book. For permission to incorporate
that material, I am grateful to the editors of *American Quarterly,*

Bulletin of the New York Public Library, Centennial Review, Concerning Poetry, Frost Centennial Essays: I, New England Quarterly, and *Prairie Schooner.*

In quoting from Frost's poetry I have relied on *Complete Poems of Robert Frost, 1949* (New York: Holt, 1949) except, obviously, in the case of poems published in *In the Clearing* (New York: Holt, Rinehart and Winston, 1962) and in two other instances, to which I draw the reader's attention in the appropriate footnotes. I have so chosen because the 1949 edition was the last "complete" edition that the poet saw through the press, and this fact in my opinion outweighs all considerations—some of them debatable at best—favoring the edition prepared by Edward Connery Lathem after the poet's death, with its many corrections, restorations, and other textual changes. It is true that Frost often made changes in poems, even after publication, but since he did not make changes in his *Complete Poems* after 1949, this edition, embodying his final intentions as best we know them, is the one to be followed.

ONE

Directives

The courteous conversing of one poem with another is
artistic response at its best.
—Richard Wilbur, "Poetry's Debt to Poetry" (1973)

THE CONCLUDING LINES of "Directive," a
poem collected in *Steeple Bush* (1947), speak imperatively to
those who have successfully made the journey back through
space and time to the brook by "a house that is no more a
house / Upon a farm that is no more a farm / And in a town that
is no more a town." "Here are your waters and your watering
place," directs the poet; "Drink and be whole again beyond
confusion."[1] Frost had drawn extensively in this poem upon
Henry David Thoreau's great New England source book, *Walden*.[2] But the most important lines in his poem, insisted Frost,
were not the concluding ones but those reading:

> Your destination and your destiny's
> A brook that was the water of the house,
> Cold as a spring as yet so near its source,
> Too lofty and original to rage.

In fact, "the key word in the whole poem is source," he concluded, "whatever source it is."[3]

As usual Frost speaks in parables, both within the poem and
elsewhere. He fully expects us to know the mythic properties of
such lost seminal places, but the quest for them, he makes clear
elsewhere in the poem, is not for just anyone. He draws on
scripture to tell us as much when he says that the "broken
drinking goblet like the Grail" is "Under a spell so the wrong
ones can't find it, / So can't get saved, as Saint Mark says they
mustn't." It is tempting (and legitimate, I think) to see in

"Directive" a parable designed by Frost so that we will infer something about his own practice as a poet. His poems have sources—buried ones—that should count for a great deal with discerning readers. To discover, for example, that *Walden* has influenced the waters that flow through Frost's own poem is to discover that Frost the questing poet has made more than the single "experienced" journey he describes in his poem. He has made a journey (if we grant him the "fiction" that he has literally walked to such a place, to a house that is no longer on a farm that is now lost and so forth) which has enabled him to "walk back" through Thoreau's recorded steps in *Walden*, both as the sojourner at Walden Pond and as the latter-day writer. Thoreau himself had returned to "sources" when he took up residence at the Pond, and he recorded that return in a book. In "Directive" we have an additional "return" in that Frost would have the "knowing" uncover the fact that his poet's hidden "source" was Thoreau's *Walden*.

In wise passivity, Thoreau's neighbor Emerson decided that "Man is a stream whose source is hidden."[4] In the face of that mystery, Frost, like Emerson, became a quester, whether for the purple fringed orchis or for some momentary "whiteness" at the bottom of an unsingular well. He would seek out that hidden place. Find the source—at least come as close to it as you can, the poet directs, then drink, and be whole again—beyond "confusion."

In response to one of the first pieces I wrote about Robert Frost's poetry, one reader remarked, "I, for one, have no doubt that Frost was really recalling those ice-bent trees back in New England." I had not denied the possibility, but I had suggested that Thoreau's description of birches during a Concord winter in his journals served to focus Frost's memory in the poem "Birches." Frost drew extensively upon Thoreau's work, not only in "Birches" but also in other poems, and profited from the work of many other writers as well. Any readers who would see Frost's poems as largely the "records" of unmediated direct experience alone—that is to say, of experience that excludes literary experience—I would direct to Frost's own theory regarding literary tradition and the individual poetic talent. As he

observed in introducing *The Arts Anthology: Dartmouth Verse,*
1925:

No one given to looking under-ground in spring can have failed to
notice how a bean starts its growth from the seed. Now the manner of a
poet's germination is less like that of a bean in the ground than of a
waterspout at sea. He has to begin as a cloud of all the other poets he
ever read. That can't be helped. And first the cloud reaches down
toward the water from above and then the water reaches up toward the
cloud from below and finally cloud and water join together to roll as one
pillar between heaven and earth. The base of water he picks up from
below is of course all the life he ever lived outside of books.[5]

The notion was much in Frost's mind that year, for he told the
editors of *Amherst Writing*, an undergraduate magazine: "Poetry
begins in reading of books and reaches down to pick up the
living of life. Individuality first shows in the poet's slant, the
way he takes his dive. We are talking of a stage further on than
conscious imitation—I have no patience with deliberately play-
ing the sedulous ape. We are talking of the person who writes
out of the eddy in his mind of all the books he ever read."[6]

In the present book I shall attempt to trace the way in which
Frost has gleaned his brain of the poems attributable to the
poetic waterspout. As earnest, let me offer an example from
Frost's prose—actually a talk that he gave in 1918 at the Browne
and Nichols School that survives because George Browne tran-
scribed it at the time. "There are two kinds of language," Frost
said familiarly, "the spoken language and the written lan-
guage—our everyday speech which we call the vernacular; and a
more literary, sophisticated, artificial, elegant language that
belongs to books."[7] Bookish language, he continues, will be
accepted by most people in the printed word but not in speech,
though he himself would prefer to do without it altogether. Yet
it is not enough to return to the speech of everyday and just stay
with it. "We've got to come down to this speech of everyday, to
begin with—the hard everyday word of the street, business,
trades, work in summer—to begin with; but there is some sort
of obligation laid on us, to lift the words of every day, to give
them a metaphorical turn."[8] Such "lifting" he later renames

4　　　　　　　　　　　　　　　　　　　　　　　　　DIRECTIVES

"fetching" and redefines as the taking of "a word or name from its place" and using it "figuratively—metaphor, simile, analogy, or allegory." The trick is to fetch a "phrase from its regular place to a new and effective place" and get "away with it." The danger, however, is that words and phrases can be fetched too far.[9] He then concludes with examples of poetically fetched words. But before looking at the last of these, I would like to reach back to the eddy from which Frost fetched his own discussion of every-day and poetic language. In *Walden* Thoreau accounts for the state of language in his day:

> It would seem as if the very language of our parlors would lose all its nerve and degenerate into *palaver* wholly, our lives pass at such re-moteness from its symbols, and its metaphors and tropes are necessarily so far fetched, through slides and dumb-waiters, as it were; in other words, the parlor is so far from the kitchen and workshop. The dinner even is only the parable of a dinner, commonly. As if only the savage dwelt near enough to Nature and Truth to borrow a trope from them. How can the scholar, who dwells away in the North West Territory or the Isle of Man, tell what is parliamentary in the kitchen?[10]

The true subject here may or may not be bookish language and everyday language, but the reader can legitimately ask in any case whether Thoreau has himself fetched his words too far. How far will the reader travel back through "slides and dumb-waiters" to recover the freshness (or better, to discover the freshness of Thoreau's fetching) in words and phrases such as "parlor," "palaver," "in other words," "parable," and "parlia-mentary"?

"The Unmade Word, or Fetching and Far-fetching" is the title of Frost's 1918 lecture at the Browne and Nichols School. Frost may not himself have chosen this title, but it is apt. At the end of his lecture he turned to one of his own poems to point out, as he put it, "one or two of these words that I 'fetched.' " He wanted the boys in his audience to consider "where I got them, where I fetched them to, and whether I fetched them too far."

> In this poem on "The Birches," I'm trying to give you the effect of a similar ice storm; the birch twigs encased in ice:

> Often you must have seen them
> Loaded with ice a sunny winter morning
> After a rain. They click upon themselves
> As the breeze rises, and turn many-colored
> As the stir cracks and crazes their enamel.

There are other words in the poem I like, but where do you think I got that word "crazes"? . . . [Mr. Frost went to the blackboard, and drew the pattern of crackly china, like the Dedham pottery.]

> Such heaps of broken glass to sweep away
> You'd think the inner dome of heaven had fallen.

I wonder if you think I fetched that word dome too far? It's not so good as the other, in spite of the "broken glass," but I like it.[11]

There are two kinds of fetching here: "crazes" from direct experience, as Frost notes, and "dome" from literary experience, which he does not mention. He could have told his students, as Richard Wilbur would later,[12] that he had fetched the word "dome" from "Adonais," Shelley's lament for Keats: "Life, like a dome of many-coloured glass, / Stains the white radiance of Eternity." The sly, deeper message of Frost's lecture on fetching and far-fetching is not only that the language of everyday usage can be fetched (success) or far-fetched (failure) for poetry but that the language used by other poets can be fetched or far-fetched by the poet (read "Frost") of everyday speech. In "Birches"—with "crazes," with "dome," and with images from Thoreau—the poet had fetched each word "from its regular place to a new and effective place, and got away with it." One can only nod in assent when Richard Wilbur writes of "Birches": "To begin with, this poem comes out of the farm and woodland country of northern New England, and everything in it is named in the right language."[13]

In writing this book I have drawn on Frost's advice about reading poetry. "A poem is best read in the light of all the other poems ever written. We read A the better to read B (we have to start somewhere; we may get very little out of A). We read B the better to read C, C the better to read D, D the better to go back and get something more out of A. Progress is not the aim, but circulation. The thing is to get among the poems where they hold each other apart in their places as the stars do."[14] Frost's poems are not, of course, read against very many of "all the other poems ever written." Rather they are read mainly against poems and essays by some of his great New England predecessors. Here I am concerned not solely with identifying the sources for Frost's poems but with demonstrating how the knowledge of sources—certain and probable—enables the reader to see the way Frost's poems hold themselves apart from the poems and texts with which they "converse" (to borrow Richard Wilbur's felicitous term).[15] Frost was concerned, it might be said, not just with the stars and the empty spaces between them, or with persistent togetherness and loneliness, but with the ratio to be established between his poems and the various texts—particularly the New England ones—with their attendant advantages and disadvantages (of the latter, relatively few).

This book, then, considers how Robert Frost fetched—sometimes from afar—from the work of predecessors such as Emerson, Thoreau, Longfellow, William James, and Emily Dickinson. Their importance to him cannot be minimized. He read Dickinson's first books when they appeared in the 1890s and was still mentioning her poems at the end of his life. Frost often spoke of Emerson; on one occasion he observed that the philosophy teachers "think Emerson is unsound but his penetrations go right through things."[16] Regarding Thoreau, suffice it to note that during Frost's final visit to the Abernethy Collection in the Middlebury College library in 1962, he said: "You know, I have come to think he was a greater one than Emerson, after all."[17] William James was Frost's great teacher because he was "the teacher I never had."[18] He paid tribute to Longfellow by taking the title of his first book from one of Longfellow's poems. This book assumes, as Emerson did, that "we are as much informed of a writer's genius by what he selects as by what he originates."[19]

PART ONE

Dickinson, Etc.

TWO

Dangling Conversation

> The two Dickinson rooms on the third floor of the Library
> are a minor Mecca for both researchers and pilgrims. The
> Library's crown of glory, however, are the Robert Frost
> rooms.
> —Frank Prentice Rand, *The Jones Library in Amherst*
> (1969)

THE FROST ROOMS in the Jones Library are high-
ceilinged, fenestrated on three sides, spacious, and ample. The
library's Dickinson rooms are spare, small, low-ceilinged, and
spottily fenestrated. That Frost inherited the better quarters can
be attributed largely, of course, to his having been a living
presence when the decisions to create and to find quarters for a
Frost Collection were made. By the time arrangements were
made for the Emily Dickinson Collection, the poet's fortunes
were in the hands of a proud niece, Martha Dickinson Bianchi,
and a few well-meaning but disorganized strangers, who were no
match for the living poet managing his own public relations.

The assignment of rooms in the Jones Library notwithstand-
ing, literary historians have often given Dickinson the greater
reputation. Frost felt fiercely competitive with his predecessors
as well as with his contemporaries, and his responses to Dickin-
son's growing popularity ranged from deference to deprecation.
Once he called her "a genius, but mad."[1] Yet in a more generous
moment, he honored her (albeit chauvinistically) as "the best of
all the women poets who ever wrote, from Sappho on down."[2]

This tribute Frost paid in 1960, at a time when he had been
deeply disappointed by Amherst College's failure to invite him
to participate in its Dickinson celebration. Throughout his life
he had read her poems as they appeared, often citing specific

poems, in conversation or on public occasions, as examples of
the kind of poetry he most favored. His choices ranged through
the canon, from "The Clouds their Backs together laid," pub-
lished in 1890, and "My life closed twice before its close,"
published in 1896, to "The Mountains—grow unnoticed," first
published in 1929.[3]

Frost's praise of Dickinson's poetry was not always un-
qualified, however. Occasionally he would grumble that she
disdained stanzaic form, rhyme, and meter. Emily Dickinson
had not studied prosody as such, of course, but still she "should
have been more careful." "She was more interested in getting
the poem down and writing a new one," he complained. "I feel
that she left some to be revised later, and she never revised
them. . . . She has all kinds of off rhymes. Some that do not
rhyme. Her meter does not always go together." Contrasting her
work with his own, he would add: "I try to make good sentences
fit the meter. That is important . . . Though I admit that Emily
Dickinson, for one, didn't do this always. When she started a
poem, it was 'Here I come!' and she came plunging through. The
meter and rhyme often had to take care of itself."[4] Sooner or
later, though, he would inevitably acknowledge that, in her
poetry, rhyme always gave way to truth; this constant force
made him "feel her strength."[5]

Despite Frost's avowed interest in Emily Dickinson, his
critics have said little about the ways in which his response to
her work might have contributed to the shape of his own early
poetry. Some affinities and interrelated differences are discerni-
ble in Frost's early poems, principally the small group published
between 1894 and 1901, and the first Dickinson poems pub-
lished in the 1890s.

Frost discovered the poetry of Emily Dickinson, just out in
two small volumes, *Poems* (1890) and *Poems, Second Series*
(1891), in the spring of 1892, during his final months at Law-
rence High School. He was immediately taken with her, dis-
covering in her poetry the voice of a kindred New England soul.
As Lawrance Thompson has written:

Although her terse, homely, gnomic, cryptic, witty qualities appealed
very strongly to him, he was again fascinated to find that this new

author was also "troubled about many things" concerning death. It seemed to him that while she had developed an extraordinary capacity for running the gamut of moods in her various imaginative confrontations with death, the poems which cut deepest for him were those which expressed her doubt whether any reasons fashioned by the mind concerning life in heaven could compensate for the heart's passionate and instinctive regrets over the transience of earthly bliss.[6]

Thompson then offers as example a Dickinson poem greatly admired by the young Frost. He first read it in *Poems* (1890).

> I reason, earth is short,
> And anguish absolute,
> And many hurt;
> But what of that?
>
> I reason, we could die:
> The best vitality
> Cannot excel decay;
> But what of that?
>
> I reason that in heaven
> Somehow, it will be even,
> Some new equation given;
> But what of that?[7]

That Frost was influenced by this poem, and particularly by Dickinson's handling of the theme of death and its aftermath, is evident in his own poem "The Birds Do Thus," which appeared in the *Independent* on August 20, 1896 (48: 1125):

> I slept all day.
> The birds do thus
> That sing a while
> At eve for us.
>
> To have you soon
> I gave away—
> Well satisfied
> To give—a day.
>
> Life's not so short
> I care to keep
> The unhappy days;
> I choose to sleep.

When the poems are juxtaposed, Frost's "The Birds Do Thus" can be read as a reply to Dickinson's poem. Her anxiety is countered by his whimsy. Whereas she decides plaintively, in her twelve-line, three-stanza poem, that "earth is short" (meaning by "earth" the human lifetime, of course) Frost answers that "Life's not so short." For Dickinson, "anguish is absolute," but Frost's advice is to sleep away "the unhappy days." Even Frost's use of the short line coincides with Dickinson's custom, but there is a difference. While Dickinson moves from two-foot to three-foot lines and back again, Frost stubbornly sticks to the greater regularity of the two-foot line.

Two years earlier, in March 1894, Frost had submitted his first poem to the *Independent.* "My Butterfly," an elegy, was accepted for publication almost by return mail,[8] though it would not appear until the issue for November 8, 1894 (46: 1429). It begins somewhat archaically:

> Thine emulous, fond flowers are dead too,
>   And the daft sun-assaulter, he
> That frighted thee so oft, is fled or dead;
>   Save only me
>   (Nor is it sad to thee),
>   Save only me.
> There is none left to mourn thee in the fields.
>   The grey grass is scarce dappled with the snow;
> Its two banks have not shut upon the river;
>   But it is long ago,
>   It seems forever,
>   Since first I saw thee glance.
> With all the dazzling other ones,
>   In airy dalliance,
> Precipitate in love,
> Tossed, tangled, whirled and whirled above,
>   Like a limp rose-wreath in a fairy dance.

Later the poem turns to the poet's personal life, and it concludes naturalistically with the evidence of the butterfly's death:

> Ah, I remember me
> How once conspiracy was rife

Against my life
(The languor of it!), and
Surging, the grasses dizzied me of thought,
The breeze three odors brought,
And a gem flower waved in a wand.
Then, when I was distraught
And could not speak,
Sidelong, full on my cheek,
What should that reckless zephyr fling
But the wild touch of your dye-dusty wing!

I found that wing withered to-day:
For you are dead, I said,
And the strange birds say.
I found it with the withered leaves
Under the eaves.

Lawrance Thompson traces "My Butterfly" to Frost's stay at Dartmouth College in 1892. The poem was inspired, writes Thompson, "by a moment which had occurred late in the fall of his few months at Dartmouth, a moment when he had found a fragile butterfly wing lying among dead leaves." The aspiring poet was not immediately able to transform his memory into poetry. "Because the delicate wing seemed to him so perfect an image, representing the brevity of life," continues Thompson, "he had been trying to build an elegy around it ever since he had left Dartmouth College."[9] What finally enabled Frost to complete his poem, however, was his reading of Emily Dickinson's butterfly poems.

In *Poems* (1890) Dickinson had written, "Some things that fly there be,— / Birds, hours, the bumble-bee: / Of these no elegy" (27). But her poems about butterflies are often, like Frost's poem, elegiac. Two poems particularly show forth as antecedents for Frost's poem. Both are from *Poems, Second Series* (1891). The first, "Two Voyagers," so entitled by Dickinson's editors, is, perhaps, the better known:

Two butterflies went out at noon
And waltzed above a stream,
Then stepped straight through the firmament
And rested on a beam;

And then together bore away
Upon a shining sea,—
Though never yet, in any port,
Their coming mentioned be.

If spoken by the distant bird,
If met in ether sea
By frigate or by merchantman,
Report was not to me. [291]

Like Frost's elegy, this poem implies extinction for the but-
terflies; but it differs from that poem in that it celebrates their
fate because of the ecstasy which precedes and accompanies
that extinction. Frost's poem ends on a more naturalistic note.

   Dickinson's "The Butterfly's Day" again deals with the fact
of extinction.

From cocoon forth a butterfly
As lady from her door
Emerged—a summer afternoon—
Repairing everywhere,

Without design, that I could trace,
Except to stray abroad
On miscellaneous enterprise
The clovers understood.

Her pretty parasol was seen
Contracting in a field
Where men made hay, then struggling hard
With an opposing cloud,

Where parties, phantom as herself,
To Nowhere seemed to go
In purposeless circumference,
As 't were a tropic show.

And notwithstanding bee that worked,
And flower that zealous blew.
This audience of idleness
Disdained them, from the sky,

Till sundown crept, a steady tide,
And men that made the hay,

> And afternoon, and butterfly,
> Extinguished in its sea. [276-77]

Frost's poem and those of Dickinson show thematic correspondences—particularly regarding the importance of flight and journey, the butterfly's dalliance with immortality, and the ephemeral nature of the individual's life cycle. There are also differences, and they suggest the difference between the accomplished poet and the talented apprentice. In two important respects "My Butterfly" is less modern than Dickinson's poem. First, its diction is slightly archaic, at best belatedly Victorian— "thine," "thee," "frighted," "oft." Second, and more characteristic, is Frost's propensity to adapt his poetic symbol to an explicitly personal allegory. In the third stanza Frost presents rather discursively his allegorical application of the butterfly's fate to his own biography. Emblemized morals subjectively presented remained common in Frost, though he would learn to handle them with great skill. That "men work together . . . whether they work together or apart," for example, is the moral toward which both butterfly and poet move in their experience of a day's mowing in another early but more accomplished poem, "The Tuft of Flowers."[10]

Frost tried his hand at still other "butterfly" poems. "Blue-Butterfly Day" concisely recounts the life of a butterfly:

> It is blue-butterfly day here in spring,
> And with these sky-flakes down in flurry on flurry
> There is more unmixed color on the wing
> Than flowers will show for days unless they hurry.
>
> But these are flowers that fly and all but sing:
> And now from having ridden out desire
> They lie closed over in the wind and cling
> Where wheels have freshly sliced the April mire.[11]

The poet's tone is wistful; these creatures are not nature's poets, though they come close: they "all but sing" as their actions presage their own deaths. It is altogether fitting, therefore, that Frost, his mind on midwinter, sees his butterflies flurrying down like snowflakes to "freshly sliced" graves in the April mud. For Frost, fragility seems to equate butterflies with snow-flakes. Even in "Stopping by Woods on a Snowy Evening," Frost echoes this theme when, playing on Dickinson's phrase "easy sweeps of sky" (115), he writes of "the sweep / Of easy wind and downy flake."

"In White," an early version of "Design," describes an even more tragic aftermath to the butterfly's (or moth's) ride of desire, however. The poem would eventually become, he explained, along with, one presumes, "My Butterfly" and possibly "The Tuft of Flowers," part of his projected " 'Moth and Butterfly' book."[12] The harsh metaphysical implication of "In White," in which the stiff white moth becomes the center of a stark tableau on a "white Heal-all" as all of nature collaborates in a ritual of death, is anticipated by Dickinson's "flippant fly upon the pane; / A spider at his trade again" (279) and in the fate of "any happy flower" (98):

> The frost beheads it at its play
> In accidental power.
> The blond assassin passes on,
> The sun proceeds unmoved
> To measure off another day
> For an approving God.

In this poem a "blond assassin"—the poet's name for "frost"—commits murder for "an approving God." Seasonal assassination, this poem insists, is a part of the all-encompassing design.

My hunch goes further: "In White" draws on still another three Dickinson poems. It expands the trace of "design" in "The Butterfly's Day" (quoted above), and it borrows, for the sake of darkening, Dickinson's identification of the spider as an artist in "Cobwebs": "The spider as an artist / Has never been employed" (512). But the tone in Frost's "In White" is closer to that of Dickinson's "The Spider":

> A spider sewed at night
> Without a light
> Upon an arc of white.
> If ruff it was of dame
> Or shroud of gnome,
> Himself, himself inform. [305]

In conflating Dickinson's "artistic" white spider and "shrouded" white moth, Frost moves away from the Dickinsonian idea of heroic extinction into a white immortality to his own emphasis upon the fated, designed convergence of whiteness and death. Echoing Dickinson's preoccupation with the color itself, "In White" ("Design") works back through "My Butterfly" to Dickinson's "From the Chrysalis" (1890):

> My cocoon tightens, colors tease,
> I'm feeling for the air;
> A dim capacity for wings
> Degrades the dress I wear.
>
> A power of butterfly must be
> The aptitude to fly,
> Meadows of majesty concedes
> And easy sweeps of sky.
>
> So I must baffle at the hint
> And cipher at the sign,
> And make much blunder, if at last
> I take the clew divine. [115]

Dickinson's guarded optimism in this poem is countered by Frost's inversion of that sentiment in both "My Butterfly" and "In White." The latter poem in particular answers Dickinson. For isn't "In White" precisely an attempt on Frost's part to "baffle at the hint / And cipher at the sign," with the added twist that Frost has chosen to take not "the clew divine" but rather the clue demonic or even the clue satanic? At best, in these poems at least, Frost answers Dickinson's trace of bright optimism with his own version of end-of-the-century naturalism.

Dickinson customarily viewed the butterfly's ephemeral day as a flight of ecstasy rather than a tragic rush toward death. Her attitude informs the core of still another of Frost's poems. His "Pod of the Milkweed" builds on her most panegyric celebration of the ephemeral butterfly's total freedom. The poet begins by "Calling all butterflies of every race / From source unknown but from no special place," and he continues in a vein that recalls Dickinson in her most festive mood. The milkweed

. . . flowers' distilled honey is so sweet
It makes the butterflies intemperate.
There is no slumber in its juice for them.
One knocks another off from where he clings.
They knock the dyestuff off each other's wings—
With thirst on hunger to the point of lust.
They raise in their intemperance a cloud
Of mingled butterfly and flower dust
That hangs perceptibly above the scene.[13]

In their sinless intemperance Frost's butterflies play out the ironic boasts of Dickinson's "I taste a liquor never brewed," and the ecstasy of these "ephemerals" again links Frost's poetry to Dickinson's. Significantly, Frost's poem does not end at this point. It swerves away from Dickinson's climactic treatment of the exuberant, soulful butterfly to the notation that the broken milkweed and exhausted butterfly are, after all, the sum and residue of that day's singular activity, for "waste was of the essence of the scheme." As the poet concludes, the hard question of "why so much / Should come to nothing" must be "fairly faced." Not content finally with Dickinson's celebration of "ephemerals," Frost directs us to look for some reason beyond the useful—and wasteful—coming together of milkweed and butterfly. "Pod of the Milkweed" takes up difficult implications—though implications not then faced by Dickinson—of poems such as "Two Voyagers" ("Two butterflies went out at noon") and "The Butterfly's Day" ("From cocoon forth a butterfly").

Emily Dickinson's poetry was useful to Frost in various ways. It constituted a source for congenial images and themes. On one occasion her poetry even provided him with a way to express his deepest love and fears. When Elinor White, not yet his wife, was away at college, Frost feared that she had fallen into, as his biographer puts it, "very lax and dangerous company."[14] Racked with forebodings that soon grew into jealousy and rage, Frost nevertheless succeeded in taming his passion sufficiently to compose a poem he called "Warning."

The day will come when you will cease to know,
The heart will cease to tell you; sadder yet,

> Tho' you say o'er and o'er what once you knew,
> You will forget, you will forget.
>
> There is no memory for what is true,
> The heart once silent. Well may you regret,
> Cry out upon it, that you have known all
> But to forget, but to forget.
>
> Blame no one but yourself for this, lost soul!
> I feared it would be so that day we met
> Long since, and you were changed. And I said then,
> She will forget, she will forget.[15]

In no way does it impugn Frost's sincerity to trace this poem
to its poetic antecedents in Dickinson. Three poems in *Poems,
Third Series* anticipate Frost's "Warning."[16] The first is the
poem beginning "Heart, we will forget him!" (483), a lyric
written from the point of view of the one who would forget; the
second is the poem that begins "There is a word / Which bears a
sword" and concludes, "'Time's sublimest target / Is a soul 'for-
got'!" (479-80). The third poem, beginning "Poor little heart!
/ Did they forget thee?" (478), with its own debt to Robert Burns
(one of Frost's favorite poets),[17] anticipates Frost's use of a re-
frain built on exact repetition within the line.

One Dickinson poem might have provided Frost with the
hint for his poem on "Revelation" as well as for two of his late
couplets. To Dickinson, God's reluctance to show Himself to
man, either directly or through his creation, symbolically or
emblematically, was at best playfully capricious and at worst
inexcusably malicious. In lines first published in 1891, she
writes:

> I know that he exists
> Somewhere, in silence.
> He has hid his rare life
> From our gross eyes.
>
> 'T is an instant's play,
> 'T is a fond ambush,
> Just to make bliss
> Earn her own surprise!
>
> But should the play
> Prove piercing earnest,

> Should the glee glaze
> In death's stiff stare,
>
> Would not the fun
> Look too expensive?
> Would not the jest
> Have crawled too far? [241]

In an "answering" poem Frost turns the situation around. Babes, not gods, play at the jest: "so with all, from babes that play / At hide-and-seek to God afar, / So all who hide too well away / Must speak and tell us where they are."[18] Frost's use of the idea of children playing at hide-and-seek with a God whose earthly presence is at best veiled becomes a means of describing the process of poetic revelation. It becomes his version of Dickinson's injunction, good for poets and gods, to "Tell all the Truth but tell it slant." Indeed, both Frost and Dickinson saw the exemplary value for the poet of God's veiled presence. "The creator of poems is quite as much interested in the problem of communication as God himself."[19]

Dickinson's idea of expensive fun and jest is evident in two gnomic poems by Frost that, taken together, "answer" Dickinson's poem. In 1936 he published the couplet: "We dance round in a ring and suppose, / But the Secret sits in the middle and knows."[20] In 1959 he had developed the matter in a proposal that pursues the Dickinsonian idea of a divine "jest": "Forgive, O Lord, my little jokes on Thee / And I'll forgive Thy great big one on me."[21]

That Emily Dickinson's poetry was often in Frost's mind during his first decade as a poet can be supported in still another way. Even when the primary source of a poem was not Dickinson, Frost still tended to cast his poem in Dickinsonian terms. A case in point is "The Quest of the Orchis," also published in the *Independent* (June 27, 1901, 53:1494):[22]

> I felt the chill of the meadow underfoot,
>   But the sun o'erhead;
> And snatches of verse and song of scenes like this
>   I sung or said.

I skirted the margin alders for miles and miles
In a sweeping line;
The day was the day by every flower that blooms,
But I saw no sign.

Yet further I went before the scythes should come,
For the grass was high;
Till I saw the path where the slender fox had come
And gone panting by.

Then at last and following that I found—
In the very hour
When the color flushed to the petals, it must have been—
The far-sought flower.

There stood the purple spires, with no breath of air
Or headlong bee
To disturb their perfect poise the livelong day
'Neath the aldertree!

I only knelt and, putting the boughs aside,
Looked, or at most
Counted them all to the buds in the copse's depth,
Pale as a ghost.

Then I arose and silent wandered home,
And I for one
Said that the fall might come and whirl of leaves
For summer was done.

Frost of course had many such "snatches of verse and song of scenes like this" available to him, for many New Englanders have written about the gentian (the flower Frost mistook for the orchis), among them William Cullen Bryant, Emerson, Thoreau, John Burroughs, and, of course, Emily Dickinson. Actually, Dickinson wrote two such attending poems, one beginning "The gentian weaves her fringes" (328-29) and another, which I reproduce below, "Fringed Gentian":

God made a little gentian;
It tried to be a rose
And failed, and all the summer laughed.
But just before the snows

> There came a purple creature
> That ravished all the hill;
> And summer hid her forehead,
> And mockery was still.
> The frosts were her condition;
> The Tyrian would not come
> Until the North evoked it.
> "Creator! shall I bloom?" [330]

Now, Frost undoubtedly encountered "Fringed Gentian" in at least two of the three places in which it appeared in the 1890s: the *Independent* (1891), *Poems, Second Series* (1891), and Mrs. William Starr Dana's *How to Know the Wild Flowers* (1893), a guidebook over which Frost pored in the 1890s.[23] It should be acknowledged that Frost's poem reflects elements of Dickinson's poems while more strongly exhibiting the influence of Emerson's "Woodnotes" and Mrs. Dana's book. If Emerson's poem describes the ideal seeker of such an elusive flower, Mrs. Dana provides directions for the search. In her book Frost found the particulars for his own poet's quest: "The fringed gentian is fickle in its habits, and the fact that we have located it one season does not mean that we will find it in the same place the following year; being a biennial, with seeds that are easily washed away, it is apt to change its haunts from time to time. So our search for this plant is always attended with the charm of uncertainty. Once having ferreted out its new abiding-place, however, we can satiate ourselves with its loveliness, which it usually lavishes unstintingly upon the moist meadows which it has elected to honor."[24] It is notable that Mrs. Dana herself had been inspired by Dickinson's own "snatch of verse" on the elusive gentian.

Frost was only moderately successful at placing his poetry in his first dozen years of trying, but it is noteworthy that his Dickinsonian poems were the first to see print. Her example had directed him to the kind of poetry that he then wanted to write and that, at least to some extent, editors wanted to put before their readers. Throughout his long career he would continue lyrically to treat certain themes that Dickinson had first put into poetic focus for him, even though he had early discovered a personal voice that would come to be associated with his major work. To Frost, Emily Dickinson's poetry always remained an example, a resource, a warning, a challenge, and, above all, a threat. He did not name her, but he probably had her in mind when late in life he insisted that one of his reasons for writing "eclogues" was "to do something women have never succeeded in doing."[25]

THREE

One Hand Clapping

You read your Emily Dickinson, and I my Robert Frost.
—Paul Simon and Art Garfunkel, "The Dangling
Conversation" (1966)

OF COURSE Robert Frost was the one they should have asked. But no one asked him. Instead the committee invited three other poets: Louise Bogan, Archibald MacLeish, and Richard Wilbur.

The occasion was the bicentennial celebration of the town of Amherst in 1959. The event was a panel discussion organized by Amherst College to honor Emily Dickinson as part of the town's festivities. Frost was miffed. To him it was a serious matter, perhaps an insult. He did not attend the panel discussion, and there is no evidence that when, a year later, the talks were collected in a slim green volume entitled *Emily Dickinson: Three Views*,[1] he ever read them. The book was not in the collection that Frost's daughter presented to New York University after his death. But Frost did vent his feelings, at least once, before the event took place. We owe a debt to Frost's friend Louis Mertins, who in his valuable book, *Robert Frost: Life and Talks—Walking*, preserved the following account of a walking talk given in the fall of 1959:

President Cole told me he had given me to the town for the bicentennial. The Jones Library belongs to the town, you know. Charlie Green's been here so long, done such a good job, people think it belongs to him. This town's grown so. I remember when we referred to the *village* of Amherst. In connection with the bicentennial, the college is featuring Emily Dickinson. I wasn't asked to be on the panel of discussion. Now some who *are* on the panel don't know too much about Emily—Archie doesn't, I know. Louise Bogan doesn't know as much as she thinks she does. The other fellow, a college man here, Richard Wilbur, isn't interested in Emily at all. If you want my opinion, she is the best of all the women poets who ever wrote, from Sappho on down. As for the other women poets—Mrs. Browning and the rest—they can't touch Emily. Really, Mrs. Browning wasn't much—greatly overrated. Emily wrote fine lines—right from the soul.[2]

This passage has the overall ring of his talks as they were transcribed at the Bread Loaf School of English in the 1950s and early 1960s and published by Reginald Cook.[3] If Mertins's transcription seems a bit too smooth for those who recall the spurts and new starts of the Bread Loaf talks, there is here, nevertheless, the sound of Frost's speaking voice, the rhythms and cross-cuts of his mind at work. If President Cole gave him to the town for the bicentennial, and if the Jones Library belongs to the town (the Frost rooms had just been dedicated), how could the college, an entity within the town, ignore him and his claim to speak out in honor of Emily? Who had better claim? Typically, to establish his own unique credentials, Frost needed to run down those who would usurp his rightful place. Archie doesn't know much about Emily Dickinson. And in a later passage of talk on the same occasion, Frost attacks MacLeish's hit play of the period, *J.B.*, with its too-facile message of love. "People think everything is solved by love," Frost sneered; "maybe just as many things are solved by hate."[4] Louise Bogan simply knows less than she thinks. And Richard Wilbur, although having a local claim, is a college man, as Frost is quick to tell us. No matter that as early as the late 1940s Frost was singling out Wilbur, along with Lowell, Shapiro, Viereck, Ciardi, and Elizabeth Bishop, as one of the very best of poets among his younger contemporaries.[5] And no matter—although such things did indeed matter to Frost—that "Dick Wilbur," as Frost once told an audience, was married to the granddaughter of William Hayes Ward, the poet-minister who edited the *Independent*, the national weekly which had first published Frost in the 1890s.[6] Moreover, Wilbur had frequently talked and written sensitively and admiringly of Frost's own poetry. As Frost once said, when you play baseball you have to "spike 'em as you go around the bases."[7]

It is not to be regretted, of course, that MacLeish, Bogan, and Wilbur were chosen for the occasion. MacLeish's measured, leisurely, but steady-gaited movement through the varied territory of Dickinson's poetry now strikes some of us as a more useful key to MacLeish's mode of thinking about poetry than to Dickinson's poems, true, but Wilbur's essay—a classic—continues to be invaluable as it clarifies Dickinson's rich but sometimes confusing poetic psyche. And as for Bogan, let it suffice to say that she must have been the first critic—and certainly the most influential to that date—to write of the poem "My Life had stood—a Loaded Gun" that it "defies analysis." "Is this an allegory," Bogan asked, "and if so of what? Is it a cry from some psychic deep where good and evil are not to be separated? In any case, it is a poem whose reverberations are infinite, as in great music; and we can only guess with what agony it was written down."[8]

What we must regret in the Amherst College bicentennial committee's decision to exclude Frost from the panel, which certainly could not have been inadvertent, is that we lost forever the opportunity to hear Frost comment at length on Emily Dickinson after nearly seventy years of reading, thinking about, and occasionally talking about her poetry. Robert Frost, as a high school senior at Lawrence High School, had known the Amherst poet's poetry almost as early as anyone else did, of course excepting the members of her immediate family, certain close friends and correspondents, one famous mentor, and Mabel Loomis Todd. He had bought the first volume of *Poems* not long after its publication in 1890 and had given his copy to his sweetheart and classmate Elinor White. And when *Poems, Second Series* appeared, he bought that too. To these volumes, over the decades, he would add other collections of her poetry as well as biographical, bibliographical, and critical books about her—the latter, admittedly, were gifts from their authors.

Let me digress for a moment to comment on Frost's Dickinson books. What remains of his collection of Dickinson books is available at New York University at the Fales Library. But neither *Poems* (1890) nor *Poems, Second Series* (1891) is there. *Poems* Frost himself gave away. "I'll tell you about Emily Dickinson's first edition with me," he once said. "Somebody was so kind to me in England—an important lady—that I gave her my first edition of Emily Dickinson." He would see the book once again before losing track of it. "The next time I was at their house I wandered into a hall and there was a little bookcase with discarded children's books. And that [the first edition of Emily Dickinson's *Poems*] was among them."⁹ *Poems, Second Series*, however, was still in Frost's possession at the time of his death, and it was subsequently transferred, along with the rest of his Cambridge library, to New York University. Unfortunately, the volume has been missing since some time before January 1975, when I first asked for it at the Fales Library.

The single most valuable Dickinson book in the Frost collection is the author's copy of *The Complete Poems of Emily Dickinson*, with an introduction by Martha Dickinson Bianchi (1924). The book was clearly not a gift from Madame Bianchi, for there was never any love lost between the two. In fact, in the war between the houses (that is, between the Dickinson/Bianchi and Todd/Bingham houses), Frost seemed to favor the house founded by Emily's brother's mistress. "For Mabel Loomis Todd," he wrote in a copy of *North of Boston*, "in part payment for her gift to us all of Emily Dickinson's poems."¹⁰ Frost's copy of the 1924 Bianchi edition of *The Complete Poems of Emily Dickinson* contains what must be presumed to be Frost's own markings in the form of slashes (one, two, or three) to the left of the first lines of some forty-eight poems. It is instructive to examine this volume, even if one can do no more than speculate on Frost's reasons for making these markings, and there are surprises. "I taste a liquor never brewed" receives one slash, "I like to see it lap the Miles" three. "I stepped from Plank to Plank" has one, "A Bird came down the Walk" two, and "A narrow Fellow in the Grass" three. "There's a certain Slant of light" earns only one slash, as do "My Cocoon tightens—Colors teaze," and, most surprising, given its affinities with some of Frost's own early poetry, "The Spider as an Artist." Some of the other choices seem even more idiosyncratic. "Because I could not stop for Death" receives one slash, for instance, but "I never saw a Moor" and "The Bustle in the House" receive three. Interestingly, "In Winter in my Room" earns three.

Whether or not these marks withstood the test of years is a

nice question. We cannot of course know for certain what common sense suggests, namely that there would inevitably be changes, with some poems demoted, others promoted, and new ones added. It is nevertheless noteworthy that "My life closed twice," which in the 1924 *Complete Poems* sports two slashes, had by the 1950s become for Frost one of Dickinson's canonical poems.

The other Dickinson-related books in the Fales Library include *Emily Dickinson, December 10, 1830–May 15, 1886: A Bibliography* (1930). This work has a foreword by George F. Whicher, who inscribed the copy "To Robert and Elinor Frost with regards[,] George F. Whicher." Some of the pages are uncut. Whicher also presented Frost with his *This Was a Poet: A Critical Biography* (1938), inscribing it: "To Robert From George With long, long thoughts [,] October, 1938." The collection also holds three other studies of Emily Dickinson. Sister Mary James Power inscribed her copy of *In the Name of the Bee* (1944): "For Robert Frost, whom I admire next to Emily D. [,] Sister Mary James." The copy is in dust jacket. Thomas H. Johnson's *Emily Dickinson: An Interpretative Biography* (1955) is also in dust jacket and contains Frost's bookplate. Genevieve Taggard's *The Life and Mind of Emily Dickinson* (1930) is inscribed: "To Eleanor and Robert Frost [,] if Emily were alive now how checked and worn your pages! Genevieve Taggard." It too is in dust jacket.

Of the Taggard book, incidentally, Frost once wrote to Louis Untermeyer: "Genevieve Taggard did awfully well, all things considered, but it is exactly as you say about her. She doesn't make a case out for her man, and she would have had more fun in making it out that there was no man at all." Indeed, Frost preferred his own theory. "In my biography," he added, "I have it that Madam Martha was Emily's neither legitimate nor illegitimate child, parthenogenetic by the composite imago of all the men it might have been."[11] In the war between Martha Dickinson Bianchi and Mabel Loomis Todd, as we have already noticed, Frost always sided with Mrs. Todd, "Emily Dickinson's brother's mistress."[12]

The student interested in Frost's relationship with his formidable New England ancestor will learn little, I suspect, from the Dickinson-related books presented to him. Even the Taggard volume is less than helpful. Of greatest value—barring, of course, the reappearance of Frost's copies of *Poems* and *Poems, Second Series*, with any markings and/or commentary that they may contain—is his list of poems in the *Complete Poems* of 1924, supplemented by a list of those Dickinson poems he is known to have mentioned as favorites or as otherwise interesting. The latter group, according to Reginald Cook and Hyde Cox,[13] includes poems such as "The Heart asks Pleasure—first" and "The Soul selects her own Society—," which appear in the 1924 *Complete Poems* but are unmarked. Two other poems also belong to this group: "Beauty—be not cause—It is," which first achieved print in 1929 in the *Saturday Review of Literature*, and "Tell all the Truth but tell it slant" (a most Frostian performance), which remained unknown until Millicent Todd Bingham published it in *Bolts of Melody* in 1945.

The student of Frost and Dickinson will of course go even further afield, beyond these instances of documented acquaintanceship, to investigate affinities, kinships, echoes, and borrowings in the seventy-year period that Frost spent coming to terms with a precursor whose technique often repelled him but whose lines, emanating from the soul, so moved him that he felt compelled to rank her among the great poets.

Still, he found it difficult to reconcile his sense of her greatness as a poet with his conviction that she did not pay sufficient attention to her craft, to matters of rhyme and meter. Her wit, insight, and cleverness—the other three elements that he once traced with approval to Mother Goose—he could apprehend with ease, but her cavalier attitude toward rhyme and metrics plagued him. Yet Dickinson's ability to bring off the miracle, letting rhyme falter and meter hang (or peter out) when it came time in a poem for truth to blazon forth ("That makes me feel her strength," he is quoted as having said),[14] caused Frost to number her among the immortal poets (and not just among the women poets, as he said to Mertins). Had he been invited to sit on the Amherst College panel in 1959, he might have accounted for this ability.

Let me suggest very briefly and roughly what he might have said. My guesses derive from some of his early complaints and from remarks he made about Emily Dickinson in the 1950s.[15]

I try to make good sentences fit the meter. That is important. Good grammar. I don't like to twist the order around in order to fit a form. I try to keep regular structure and good rhymes. Though I admit that Emily Dickinson, for one, didn't do this always. When she started a poem it was "Here I come!"—and she came plunging through. The meter and rhyme often had to take care of itself. Still, there's the matter of sound, the sound a sentence makes, depending as it does on a poet's and his reader's having heard the intonations of the words—a sound which lies behind the sense the words of a sentence, taken at face value, add up to. I say you can't read a single good sentence with the salt in it unless you have previously heard it spoken. Words exist in the mouth, not in books. Take Emily Dickinson's poetry. Here's the first stanza of a poem that shows how she got the sound of sense into her lines:

> *The mountains grow unnoticed,*
> *Their purple figures rise*
> *Without attempt, exhaustion,*
> *Assistance or applause.*

Never mind that "rise/applause" slant rhyme, and pass over the assonance in the last line. These are strong lines, but there's a better strength than jettisoning the rhymes.

But those missing, missed rhymes—a nail in the shoe. Emily Dickinson is a poet who never gets sidetracked. She wrote without thought of publication and was not under the necessity of revamping and polishing; it was easy for her to go right to the point and say just what she thought and felt. Her technical irregularities give her poems strength, as if she were saying, "Look out, Rhyme and Meter, here I come." I like this willfulness, this unmanageability of the thought, by the form; but it does seem to be a little too easily arrived at by Emily Dickinson where at times it's indistinguishable from carelessness. Sometimes she gives up the technical struggle too soon. But then there's the importance of noticing in life—in reading, in scholarship, in poetry. The most noticing man that ever lived maybe was Thoreau, wasn't he? He noticed some things wrong, they like to point out. But he was a very noticing man. So was Emily Dickinson. No point in saying, though, that she was greater than Thoreau, as Conrad Aiken once said. There's no need for such "invidious comparisons." It's enough to see what she took notice of. Take the line, "The Lightning skipped like mice." Nobody ever noticed that before. There's a whole "play of ideas" in that that's as good as Mother Goose:

> Pussy cat, pussy cat, where have you been?
> I've been to London to see the Coronation!

To pervert a little:

> Pussy cat, pussy cat, what did you see there?
> I saw nothing but what I might have seen just
> As well by staying right here at home.
> I saw a mouse run under a chair.

And that's very deep. But it's so pretty the way it's set off, you know, and nobody need see it at all unless they're discerning. "I saw a mouse run under a chair." That's meant a lot to me, that has, all my life . . . . That's what makes regionalists, you see. You could stay right at home and see it all: the mice run under the chair, and the lightning skips like mice. Fresh observation, which belongs to poetry. All the time, little insights.

And then there's the high use of language. Emerson had it. I don't mean his prose. I don't mean his saying that these sentences bleed when you cut them—that was a good sentence to say, wasn't it? No, I mean, what I mean is high poetic use. Try Keats. Two words in Keats were terribly deep to me, and I get to suspecting one of them as a word that has dominated English literature for a hundred years after it. "She stood in tears amid the alien corn." And that is such a high poetic use of that word "alien" that it just got to all the poets that wrote for a hundred years. . . . This "wild surmise" (that's from another Keats poem) is another wonder. How deep that goes! I suppose I never said that word, ran through that—"Look'd at each other with a wild surmise—/Silent, upon a peak in Darien"—without something so beyond any symbolism or anything like that, or echoes, just as over some deep hollow in my nature. In poetry and under emotion every word used is "moved" a little or much—moved from its old place, heightened, *made new. See, that's what Keats did to "alien" and, joined, "wild surmise." You know, if books of verse were indexed by lines first in importance, lines carried by the high poetic use of words, our anthologies would be very different from what they are now. And Emily Dickinson would make a strong showing. Here's an example. Think of a little poem. Let's see. "My life closed twice before its close / It yet remains to see / If Immortality unveil / A third event to me, / So huge, so hopeless to conceive / As these that twice befell. / Parting is all we know of heaven, / And all we need of hell." I've mauled it a little, calling it up. Now, when you stop to look at that, does anything more than the thing itself occur to you? One can say always that some days nothing more than the thing itself occurs to you. It's huge (enough) just in itself to take. Sometimes something extra occurs to you. I remember one of the bitter ones in Amherst saying that nobody in the whole life of America made a line like "If Immortality unveil / A third event to me." The beauty of that, it occurs to me, is that she said, "My life closed twice before its close: / It yet remains to see." Now she doesn't say "death" in there. It's the way—it's the curious use, the brilliant use, the high poetic use of the word immortality. I agree to that. That's very high. Then the last two lines—"Parting is all we know of heaven, / And all we need of hell"—are wonderful epigrams. But did you ever notice as you said it that parting is all we know of heaven? What do you know of heaven? You only know that some people go there. She means "know." And all we "need" of hell. That's another word, you see. She doesn't say know of hell; she says "need." Wonderful, that "need" in there. Sometimes you get a thing like that in your head and it dawns on you. You don't want somebody to tell you about it. And by the way, notice the rhymes: "See" and "me," "befell" and "hell." Any questions? I'll read you a poem. It goes back to Mountain Interval. There was one once who would correct the use of that word—"interval." He thought I'd made a mistake, that the word was "intervale." I had to explain that the original word was "interval" ("VAL" as in "VALentine"), that "intervale," with its present pronunciation and meaning, arose from a mistake. I wrote that all out in a letter at the time. The poem—the poem from Mountain Interval that I'm going to read—is no longer than a metaphor, a little metaphor that clinches its own metaphor at the end.*

By June, our brook's run out of song and speed.
Sought for much after that, it will be found
Either to have gone groping underground
(And taken with it all the Hyla breed
That shouted in the mist a month ago,
Like ghost of sleigh-bells in a ghost of snow)—
Or flourished and come up in jewel-weed,
Weak foliage that is blown upon and bent
Even against the way its waters went.
Its bed is left a faded paper sheet
Of dead leaves stuck together by the heat—
A brook to none but who remember long.
This as it will be seen is other far
Than with brooks taken otherwhere in song.
We love the things we love for what they are.

"And he likes having thought of it so well he says again," to quote
the poet, "We love the things we love for what they are."

FOUR

Designs

The perch swallows the grub-worm, the pickerel swallows the perch, and the fisherman swallows the pickerel; and so all the chinks in the scale of being are filled.
—Henry David Thoreau, *Walden* (1854)

LECTURING IN 1834 on the theme of man's relationship to the globe, Ralph Waldo Emerson remarked:

The snail is not more accurately adjusted to his shell than man to the globe he inhabits; that not only a perfect symmetry is discoverable in his limbs and senses between the head and the foot, between the hand and the eye, the head and the lungs,—but an equal symmetry and proportion is discoverable between him and the air, the mountains, the tides, the moon, and the sun. I am not impressed by solitary marks of designing wisdom; I am thrilled with delight by the choral harmony of the whole. Design! It is all design. It is all beauty. It is all astonishment.[1]

With this notion Emerson started hares in New England that have run from his time well into the twentieth century. In Emerson's day Oliver Wendell Holmes produced his variation on the theme, seeing it in terms of what might be called Platonic evolutionism in his poem "The Chambered Nautilus." Early in this century Frost took up Emerson's notion in two versions of the poem "Design" and had serious fun with it for a decade.

Published rather inauspiciously in the same year as T. S. Eliot's "The Waste Land," Frost's sonnet "Design" has weathered the years successfully. Its reputation has grown to such an extent that the poem, like Eliot's, is now considered one of the century's most explosive poetic statements on the metaphysics of darkness. Indeed, historically "Design" can be located somewhere between the visionary expanse of "The Waste Land" and the mind-stretching speculations of Herman Melville's chapter "The Whiteness of the Whale" in *Moby-Dick* (1851). In paradigm, "Design" expresses the perplexing fears that respond to evidence that (1) human existence continues without supportive design and ultimate purpose and (2) human existence is subject to a design of unmitigated natural evil. In its details the poem appears to sustain both of these complementary interpretations.

"Design" is Frost's most carefully shaped investigation of the darker implications of the classical argument from design. The poem did not spring into being fully formed after a single bout with the Muse. In 1912, apparently to put the poem on record as well as to try it on a sympathetic reader, Frost forwarded an early version to an old friend, calling it a sonnet for his " 'Moth and Butterfly' book."[2] Although he did not choose to publish this early version, the manuscript copy preserved among the papers of Susan Hayes Ward enables us to trace Frost's philosophical-aesthetic development as he reworked the draft and rethought his ideas over a period of ten years.

Frost's extant manuscript version of 1912 bears the title "In White," which, though it indicates the poem's principal image and motif, does not have the thematic resonance of the simpler and more direct later title, "Design."[3] A more explicit, if far less effective, title for the later version of the poem might combine the two: "Design in White." Still, this title, arty and somewhat arch, would compromise Frost's theme. Rather, concerned with any and all designs which would foster poetic and philosophic resonance, Frost revised his poem to make it more precise, so that each image would be appropriate and every word functional.

> In White
> A dented spider like a snow drop white
> On a white Heal-all, holding up a moth
> Like a white piece of lifeless satin cloth—
> Saw ever curious eye so strange a sight?—
> Portent in little, assorted death and blight
> Like the ingredients of a witches' broth?—
> The beady spider, the flower like a froth,
> And the moth carried like a paper kite.

> What had that flower to do with being white,
> The blue prunella every child's delight.
> What brought the kindred spider to that height?
> (Make we no thesis of the miller's plight.)
> What but design of darkness and of night?
> Design, design! Do I use the word aright?[4]

This early version of the poem is to be compared with the final version published first in 1922 and later gathered by Frost into his sixth volume of poetry, *A Further Range* (1936):

> I found a dimpled spider, fat and white,
> On a white heal-all, holding up a moth
> Like a white piece of rigid satin cloth—
> Assorted characters of death and blight
> Mixed ready to begin the morning right,
> Like the ingredients of a witches' broth—
> A snow-drop spider, a flower like a froth,
> And dead wings carried like a paper kite.

> What had that flower to do with being white,
> The wayside blue and innocent heal-all?
> What brought the kindred spider to that height,
> Then steered the white moth thither in the night?
> What but design of darkness to appall?—
> If design govern in a thing so small.[5]

Frost's revisions turn the poem to narrative and away from unadorned lyric, thereby enhancing the mystery that surrounds the incident he wishes to describe. In removing his personal experience to the past, the poet is able to suggest as well that he has been brooding on the meaning of the tableau of spider, moth, and ritual death which he has observed, even though he has failed to reach a conclusive answer (at least for himself) on the question of design. The introduction of the poet's personal voice (as subject) into the first line, moreover, turns the spider into the obect of sight and contemplation. It gives the poet more prominence than he had in the manuscript version, which begins with a sentence fragment (no verb) in apposition to the noun "sight" in the fourth line.

Little survives intact from one version of the poem to the

other. Notably, only the ninth line of the early version—"What had that flower to do with being white"—survives without change in "Design." Lines 2, 6, and 11 are largely repeated, with changes only in capitalization or punctuation at the end of the line. The remaining ten lines, however, offer substantive changes, which must be taken up line by line.

The simile in the first line, "like a snow drop white," which is purely and neutrally descriptive, disappears along with another descriptive word, "dented." In their place Frost offers three adjectives: "dimpled," "fat," and "white." The first two are unexpectedly appropriate for this murderous spider. Cleverly placed in the poem, these terms more often describe a baby than an insect. By replacing neutrally descriptive terms with terms that would normally appear in another context in connection with a different sentiment, Frost both announces his theme and reveals that his approach is basically ironic. In line 3 the moth, described as "a white piece of lifeless cloth" becomes "rigid satin cloth." "Lifeless" is only vaguely descriptive of the moth's state; but it does not at all accurately reflect the tableau of the spider holding up the moth. The moth may in fact be "lifeless," but the poem is more accurately descriptive when it compares the moth with "rigid" cloth. Hovering over this image is the hint of rigor mortis and the satin fabric which customarily lines the inside of coffins.[6]

Line 4 in the manuscript version is rather limp, lifeless. The semirhetorical question "Saw ever curious eye so strange a sight?" seriously deflects the central argument of the poem. In the final version Frost moves the second half of the original fifth line, "assorted death and blight," to line 4 and extends it to "assorted characters of death and blight," thereby introducing the important metaphor of kitchen domesticity that he will pursue through line 7. So, too, does he decide to drop the first phrase of line 5 ("Portent in little")—this time, I would suggest, because "portent" is too potent at this point. Line 6 stays almost intact but no longer asks a question. Indeed, the two questions which dominate the octave in the manuscript version are strategically dropped, so that the only questions come in the sestet closing the poem. Lines 4 through 7 are intended, then, to suggest kitchens, cakes, and cookies ("Assorted," "ingredients," and "Mixed ready")—all as if drummed up by advertisers "to begin the morning right." The only sour note is that the whole thing resembles "the ingredients of a witches' broth." Still, it is "broth" and not "brew" (as we might expect in everyday witchcraft); "broth" echoes the culinary metaphor.

The single change in line 7 turns "beady spider" into "snow-drop spider," reinstating the adjective which Frost had discarded from his original first line. At this point the earlier poem was still fundamentally descriptive, but something was needed, apparently to keep the idea of coldness and death before us. "Snow-drop" accomplishes this aim. "Beady," however, serves another purpose. The word, less than precisely descriptive, is morally loaded. A seemingly less neutral word would keep the poem from becoming at all moralistic. In the last line of the octave "moth" turns into "dead wings," but the simile "like a paper kite" is happily retained. The simile returns us to the implicitly "childlike" description of the spider in the opening line. "Dead wings," on the other hand, moves toward precision, for it is not the "moth" in its entirety that looks like "a paper kite" but only its "dead wings." Furthermore, both "wings" and "kite" suggest the idea of flight; the image of white "dead wings" moves toward paradox.

The ninth line ("What had that flower to do with being white,") remains intact; this much about his basic poem Frost had been sure of all along. But if the appositive clause which constitutes the tenth line ("The blue prunella every child's delight") adds the new information that the heal-all is also known as the prunella, it nevertheless adds nothing to the argument of the poem. Indeed, because the content of the lines is not at all functional except as a bit of incidental information, it can do no more than disrupt the poem's discourse. On the other hand, repetition of the fact that it is a "heal-all" despite its not being blue (as are most heal-alls) pushes the argument a step further. The next line is substantially the same. But the twelfth line of the manuscript version is dropped completely, and fittingly so. "(Make we not thesis of the miller's plight)" is wasteful and repetitive, seeming to exist only for the final word ("plight"), which maintains the pattern of the same end rhyme throughout the six lines of the sestet. In replacing the entire line, Frost chooses to deepen the question he asks about the tableau he has witnessed. Not only does he ask "What brought the kindred spider to that height" but also what "Then *steered* the *white* moth thither in the *night*?" (italics added). What power, then, actually "steered" the moth (white) in the darkness of "night" to a heal-all which is preternaturally "white"? Rather than the somewhat disingenuous admonition that avoids making a thesis out of this tableau, Frost chooses to extend the mystery of the "witches' broth" that he has ostensibly witnessed.[7]

In the penultimate line of the poem the first five words are retained ("What but design of darkness"), but the last three words ("and of night") are revised: "to appall?" In the original, "of night" merely repeats the idea in the phrase "of darkness." There is a relatively pointless, if harmless, repetition of meaning. But the phrase "darkness to appall" suggests the appalling effect that the close conjunction of two ideas—"darkness" and "design"—might well have. Moreover, "appall" is a particularly suitable word, in that it suggests both a specific color or the lack of color (pallor) and death (pall).

Because it, too, is inconclusive and somewhat wasteful, the last line of the manuscript poem gives way to a conditional clause in the final version. "Design, design! Do I use the word aright?" is crudely rhythmic, but the simple device of ending a poem with a disingenuous question does little to resolve the poem formally. On the other hand, to end the poem with the tentative clause "if design govern in a thing so small" offers thematic resolution even as it enhances poetic resonance. "Govern" develops from "steered," of course, which in turn grows out of "brought." The effect is cumulative.

A comparison of the earlier and the definitive versions of "Design" helps to define the poet's final intention; it remained fundamentally consistent. From version to version Frost worked to clarify his idea that the philosophical argument from design was endemically ironic. Both the first published version of the poem (1922) and the manuscript version (1912) are in sonnet form. Despite internal revisions and the reshaping of several lines, the overall poetic form remained the same over the years. That the poem was conceived in the form of a sonnet, I would

propose, is the poet's final irony, for the strict formal design
which characterizes the sonnet apes and mimes the internal
argument of the poem. It is true of "Design," as it is, according
to Frost, of all his poems: "every single one of the poems has its
design symbol." The difficulty, though, is that "there are some
people who want to know what's eating you."[8] Whether what is
eating at the readers of "Design" was also eating the poet is not
revealed. But here are the main questions. Does the same guid-
ing power, the steering force, which works through the tableau
of spider, moth, and stylized death, operate through the poetic
process as well? After so much whiteness, have we experienced,
after all, still another variant of that scriptural blackness of
darkness which fascinated so many American writers, from Poe
to Hemingway? These questions—good ones, I think—are no
more rhetorical than the question which closes Frost's chilling
sonnet.

There is a footnote to the story of "In White" and "Design."
It involves Frost's dealings with the *Independent*, particularly
with Susan Hayes Ward, the literary editor of the publication
edited by her brother William Hayes Ward. She was one of the
people he later singled out as having had so much to do with his
career that he would name her as one of those "to whom I owe
my existence."[9] In 1894 Frost sent the poem "My Butterfly" to
the *Independent* because two years earlier he had recognized the
journal as a place where poetry might be published. The discov-
ery was, he revealed, one of the two most crucial poetic experi-
ences in his life as a student. (The other was his discovery of
Palgrave's *Golden Treasury*.) Elizabeth Shepley Sergeant quotes
Frost:

I happened into the old library, and found on the magazine rack a copy of
the *Independent*, with a poem on the front page. It was a sort of
threnody called "Seaward," by Richard Hovey, a friend of Bliss Carman
and a celebrated Dartmouth graduate. The subject was the death of
Thomas William Parsons, translator of Dante's *Inferno*, friend of Long-
fellow.

This experience gave me my very first revelation that a publication
existed, anywhere in my native land, that was a vehicle for the publica-
tion of poetry. There was even an editorial about this poem, which I read
with rapt amaze. So when later I had a poem, "My Butterfly," I of course
sent it to the *Independent*.[10]

The issue of the *Independent* containing Hovey's poem appeared on November 17, 1892.

Almost two decades later, on about January 15, 1912, Frost sent Susan Hayes Ward a copy of "In White." By this time she was no longer associated with the *Independent* and was, in fact, retired. (She died in 1916.) Therefore, why did Frost choose to send her this particular poem? My guess is that it had something to do with poems he had read in the *Independent* years earlier, in an issue published on December 15, 1892, four weeks after the issue publishing the Hovey poem that had so favorably impressed the young would-be poet then studying at Dartmouth. In this, largely a Christmas issue, Frost would have read a twenty-two-line poem by Julian Hawthorne:

> As when a traveler, toiling o'er a hight
>   Heaped of huge bowlders, all at random hurled,
>   Like fragments of a ruined world,
> Whose desolation doth the spirit affright—
> Rebels at seeming chaos come again,
> And longs for level reaches of the plain;
>   So I with hardship spent,
>   And foiled of mine intent,
> Complained that life was less than kind,
> That silver clouds were leaden-lined,
> And chance, not justice, did o'er mortal fortunes reign.
>
> But when the traveler to the valley came,
>   And, turning, gazed at that dim-towering hight,
>   Glorified now by sunset light,—
> Lo! the confusion that had won his blame
> Assumed sublime and awful grace—
> The mighty semblance of a God-like face.
>   Even, so as I look back
>   Upon my weary track,
> I see its hostile features change,
> By some divine enchantment strange,
> Till God's design through all, in all, at last I trace.[11]

Frost's "My Butterfly," written two years later, would also touch on the "awful grace" of God's power and design: "It seemed God let thee flutter from his gentle clasp: / Then, fearful he had let thee win / Too far beyond him to be gathered in, / Snatched

thee, o'er-eager, with ungentle grasp."[12] Along with Julian
Hawthorne's "Design," however, the *Independent* for December
15, 1892, published a forty-line poem by Lewis Morris entitled
"From an American Sermon." I shall quote not the entire poem
but only two stanzas from the middle and the two at the end:

> So every human soul
> Set here betwixt its twin eternities
> Stands open to heaven, ay, rolls on to doom
> Mid opposite mysteries.

> And tho indeed it seem
> By narrow walls of circumstance confined,
> Shut from Heaven's face, closed to all vital airs,
> Is open to God's wind.
> . . . .

> No soul so cold or calm
> But underneath it burns the infernal fire
> No state so mean, so vile,
> It may not to the Heaven of heavens aspire.

> Above, beneath, around,
> Dread destinies encompass great and small;
> One Will, one Hand, one dread all-seeing Eye
> Surveys and governs all.[13]

The second of these stanzas Frost would echo dramatically
(with a hint from Emily Dickinson) in "My Butterfly": "Then,
when I was distraught / And could not speak, / Sidelong, full on
my cheek, / What should that reckless zephyr fling / But the
wild touch of your dye-dusty wing!"[14] The last stanza of Mor-
ris's poem was later echoed in "Design." It is curious that when
Frost revised "In White" he changed the poem's last line from
"Design, design! Do I use the word aright?" to "If design govern
in a thing so small," thereby echoing the last lines of both
Hawthorne's and Morris's poems. Small wonder, then, that,
when Frost came upon William James's naturalistic and anec-
dotal critique of the argument from design,[15] he was well
primed for it—from reading Hawthorne and Morris no less than
from writing "My Butterfly."

One last point is noteworthy. When Frost sent his trenchant

criticism of the argument from design ("In White) to his old benefactress, Susan Hayes Ward—especially since she was by then no longer in a position to help him with publication—was he not formally, if belatedly, answering poetic voices heard nearly two decades earlier (a settling of the score, so to speak)?

FIVE

Roads and Paths

> When a man thinks happily, he finds no foot-track in the field he traverses.
> —Ralph Waldo Emerson, "Quotation and Originality" (1859)

"THE ROAD NOT TAKEN" can be read against a literary and pictorial tradition that might be called "The Choice of the Two Paths," reaching not only back to the Gospels and beyond them to the Greeks but to ancient English verse as well.[1] In *Reson and Sensuallyte*, for example, John Lydgate explains how he dreamt that Dame Nature had offered him the choice between the Road of Reason and the Road of Sensuality. In art the same choice was often represented by the letter "Y," with the trunk of the letter representing the careless years of childhood and the two paths branching off at the age when the child is expected to exercise discretion. In one design the "Two Paths" are shown in great detail. "On one side a thin line of pious folk ascend a hill past several churches and chapels, and so skyward to the Heavenly City where an angel stands proffering a crown. On the other side a crowd of men and women are engaged in feasting, music, love-making, and other carnal pleasures while close behind them yawns the flaming mouth of hell in which sinners are writhing. But hope is held out for the worldly, for some avoid hell and having passed through a dark forest come to the rude huts of Humility and Repentance."[2] Embedded in this quotation is a direct reference to the opening of Dante's *Inferno:*

> Midway upon the journey of our life
> I found myself within a forest dark,
> For the straightforward pathway had been lost.

> Ah me! how hard a thing it is to say
>   What was the forest savage, rough, and stern,
>   Which in the very thought renews the fear.
> So bitter is it, death is little more.[3]

From the beginning, when it appeared as the first poem in *Mountain Interval* (1916), many readers have overstated the importance of "The Road Not Taken" to Frost's work. Alexander Meiklejohn, president of Amherst College, did so when, announcing the appointment of the poet to the school's faculty, he recited it to a college assembly.

> Two roads diverged in a yellow wood,
> And sorry I could not travel both
> And be one traveler, long I stood
> And looked down one as far as I could
> To where it bent in the undergrowth;
>
> Then took the other, as just as fair,
> And having perhaps the better claim,
> Because it was grassy and wanted wear;
> Though as for that the passing there
> Had worn them really about the same,
>
> And both that morning equally lay
> In leaves no step had trodden black.
> Oh, I kept the first for another day!
> Yet knowing how way leads on to way,
> I doubted if I should ever come back.
>
> I shall be telling this with a sigh
> Somewhere ages and ages hence:
> Two roads diverged in a wood, and I—
> I took the one less traveled by,
> And that has made all the difference.[4]

"The Choice of Two Paths" is suggested in Frost's decision to make his two roads not very much different from one another, for passing over one of them had the effect of wearing them "really about the same." This is a far cry from, say, the description of the "two waies" offered in the seventeenth century by Henry Crosse:

Two waies are proposed and laide open to all, the one inviting to vertue, the other alluring to vice; the first is combersome, intricate, untraded, overgrowne, and many obstacles to dismay the passenger; the other plaine, even beaten, overshadowed with boughes, tapistried with flowers, and many objects to feed the eye; now a man that lookes but only to the outward shewe, will easily tread the broadest pathe, but if hee perceive that this smooth and even way leads to a neast of Scorpions: or a litter of Beares, he will rather take the other though it be rugged and unpleasant, than hazard himselfe in so great a daunger.[5]

Frost seems to have deliberately chosen the word "roads" rather than "waies" or "paths" or even "pathways." In fact, on one occasion when he was asked to recite his famous poem, "Two paths diverged in a yellow wood," Frost reacted with such feeling—"Two *roads*!"—that the transcription of his reply made it necessary both to italicize the word "roads" and to follow it with an exclamation point. Frost recited the poem all right, but, as his friend remembered, "he didn't let me get away with 'two paths!' "[6]

Convinced that the poem was deeply personal and directly self-revelatory, Frost's readers have insisted on tracing the poem to one or the other of two facts of Frost's life when he was in his late thirties. (At the beginning of the *Inferno* Dante is thirty-five, "midway on the road of life," notes Charles Eliot Norton.)[7] The first of these, an event, took place in the winter of 1911–1912 in the woods of Plymouth, New Hampshire, while the second, a general observation and a concomitant attitude, grew out of his long walks in England with Edward Thomas, his newfound Welsh-English poet-friend, in 1914.

In *Robert Frost: The Trial by Existence,* Elizabeth Shepley Sergeant locates in one of Frost's letters the source for "The Road Not Taken." To Susan Hayes Ward the poet wrote on February 10, 1912:

Two lonely cross-roads that themselves cross each other I have walked several times this winter without meeting or overtaking so much as a single person on foot or on runners. The practically unbroken condition of both for several days after a snow or a blow proves that neither is much travelled. Judge then how surprised I was the other evening as I came down one to see a man, who to my own unfamiliar eyes and in the dusk looked for all the world like myself, coming down the other, his approach to the point where our paths must intersect being so timed that unless one of us pulled up we must inevitably collide. I felt as if I was going to meet my own image in a slanting mirror. Or say I felt as we slowly converged on the same point with the same noiseless yet laborious stride as if we were two images about to float together with the uncrossing of someone's eyes. I verily expected to take up or absorb this other self and feel the stronger by the addition for the three-mile journey home. But I didn't go forward to the touch. I stood still in wonderment and let him pass by; and that, too, with the fatal omission of not trying to find out by a comparison of lives and immediate and remote interests what could have brought us by crossing paths to the same point in a wilderness at the same moment of nightfall. Some purpose I doubt not, if we could but have made out. I like a coincidence almost as well as an incongruity.[8]

This portentous account of meeting "another" self (but not encountering that self directly and therefore not coming to terms with it) would eventually result in a poem quite different from "The Road Not Taken" and one that Frost would not publish for decades. Elizabeth Sergeant ties the moment with Frost's decision to go off at this time to some place where he could devote more time to poetry. He had also, she implies, filed away his dream for future poetic use.

That poetic use would occur three years later. In 1914 Frost arrived in England for what he then thought would be an extended sabbatical leave from farming in New Hampshire. By all the signs he was ready to settle down for a long stay. Settling in Gloucestershire, he soon became a close friend of Edward Thomas. Later, when readers persisted in misreading "The Road Not Taken," Frost insisted that his poem had been intended as a sly jest at the expense of his friend and fellow poet. For Thomas had invariably fussed over irrevocable choices of the most minor sort made on daily walks with Frost in 1914, shortly before the writing of the poem. Later Frost insisted that in his case the line "And that has made all the difference"—taken straight—was all wrong. "Of course, it hasn't," he persisted, "it's just a poem, you know."[9] In 1915, moreover, his sole intention was to twit Thomas. Living in Gloucestershire, writes Lawrance Thompson, Frost had frequently taken long countryside walks with Thomas.

Repeatedly Thomas would choose a route which might enable him to show his American friend a rare plant or a special vista; but it often happened that before the end of such a walk Thomas would regret the choice he had made and would sigh over what he might have shown Frost if they had taken a "better" direction. More than once, on such occasions, the New Englander had teased his Welsh-English friend for those wasted regrets. . . . Frost found something quaintly romantic in sighing over what might have been. Such a course of action was a road never taken by Frost, a road he had been taught to avoid.[10]

If we are to believe Frost and his biographer, "The Road Not Taken" was intended to serve as Frost's gentle jest at Thomas's expense. But the poem might have had other targets. One such target was a text by another poet who in a different sense might also be considered a "friend": Henry Wadsworth Longfellow, whose poem, "My Lost Youth," had provided Frost with A Boy's Will, the title he chose for his first book.

"The Road Not Taken" can be placed against a passage in Longfellow's notebooks: "Round about what is, lies a whole mysterious world of might be,—a psychological romance of possibilities and things that do not happen. By going out a few minutes sooner or later, by stopping to speak with a friend at a corner, by meeting this man or that, or by turning down this street instead of the other, we may let slip some great occasion of good, or avoid some impending evil, by which the whole current of our lives would have been changed. There is no possible solution to the dark enigma but the one word, 'Providence.' "[11]

Longfellow's tone in this passage is sober, even somber, and anticipates the same qualities in Edward Thomas, as Frost so clearly perceived. Elizabeth Shepley Sergeant had insisted that Frost's dream encounter with his other self at a crossroads in the woods had a "subterranean connection" with the whole of "The Road Not Taken," especially with the poem's last lines:

> I shall be telling this with a sigh
> Somewhere ages and ages hence:

> Two roads diverged in a wood, and I—
> I took the one less traveled by,
> And that has made all the difference.

Undoubtedly. But whereas Longfellow had invoked Providence to account for acts performed and actions not taken, Frost calls attention only to the role of human choice. A second target was the notion that "whatever choice we make, we make at our peril." The words just quoted are Fitz-James Stephen's, but it is more important that Frost encountered them in William James's essay "The Will to Believe." In fact, James concludes his final paragraph on the topic: "We stand on a mountain pass in the midst of whirling snow and blinding mist, through which we get glimpses now and then of paths which may be deceptive. If we take the wrong road we shall be dashed to pieces. We do not certainly know whether there is any right one. What must we do? 'Be strong and of a good courage.' Act for the best, hope for the best, and take what comes. . . . If death ends all, we cannot meet death better."[12] The danger inherent in decision, in this brave passage quoted with clear-cut approval by the teacher Frost "never had," does not play a part in "The Road Not Taken." Frost the "leaf-treader" will have none of it, though he will not refuse to make a choice. Nothing will happen to him through default. Nor, argues the poet, is it likely that anyone will melodramatically be dashed to pieces.

It is useful to see Frost's projected sigh as a nudging criticism of Thomas's characteristic regrets, to note that Frost's poem takes a sly poke at Longfellow's more generalized awe before the notion of what might have happened had it not been for the inexorable workings of Providence, and to see "The Road Not Taken" as a bravura tossing off of Fitz-James Stephen's mountainous and meteorological scenario. We can also project the poem against a poem by Emily Dickinson that Frost had encountered twenty years earlier in *Poems, Second Series* (1891).

> Our journey had advanced;
> Our feet were almost come
> To that odd fork in Being's road,
> Eternity by term.

Our pace took sudden awe,
Our feet reluctant led.
Before were cities, but between,
The forest of the dead.

Retreat was out of hope,—
Behind, a sealed route,
Eternity's white flag before,
And God at every gate.[13]

Dickinson's poem is straightforwardly and orthodoxically religious. But it can be seen that beyond the "journey" metaphor Dickinson's poem employs diction—"road" and "forest"—that recalls "The Choice of the Two Paths" trope, the opening lines of the *Inferno*, and Frost's secular poem "The Road Not Taken."

The "dark forest" in the tradition of "The Choice of the Two Paths" and the "forest dark" of Longfellow's translation of the *Inferno* also foreshadow the imagery of the famous Frost poem published in *New Hampshire* (1923), the last stanza of which begins: "The woods are lovely, dark and deep."[14] In spurning the word "forest" for "woods," a term that is perhaps more appropriate for New England, Frost was, whether he knew it or not, following Charles Eliot Norton, whose translation of the *Inferno* reads "dark wood" and who glosses the opening of Dante's poem: "The dark wood is the forest of the world of sense, 'the erroneous wood of this life' . . . , that is, the wood in which man loses his way."[15] In "the darkest evening of the year," the New England poet finds himself standing before a scene he finds attractive enough to make him linger. Frost's poem employs, significantly, the present tense. Dante's poem (through Longfellow) employs the past tense. It is as if Frost were casually remembering some familiar engraving that hung on a schoolroom wall in Lawrence as he was growing up in the 1880s, and the poet slides into the picture. He enters, so to speak, the mind of the figure who speaks the poem, a figure whose body is slowly turned into the scene, head fully away from the foreground, bulking small, holding the reins steadily and loosely. The horse and team are planted, though poised to move. And so begins the poet's dramatization of this rural and parochial tableau. "Whose

woods these are I think I know. / His house is in the village
though. / He will not see me stopping here / To watch his
woods fill up with snow." And then, having entered the human
being, he witnesses the natural drift of that human being's
thoughts to the brain of his "little horse," who thinks it "queer"
that the rider has decided to stop here. And then, in an equally
easy transition, the teamster returns to himself, remembering
that he has promises to keep and miles to go before he sleeps.
Duties, responsibilities—many must have them, we think, as
echolalia closes the poem, all other thoughts already turning
away from the illustration on the schoolroom wall. And even as
the "little horse" has been rid of the man's intrusion, so too
must the rider's mind be freed of the poet's incursion. The poet's
last line resonates, dismissing the reader from his, the poet's,
dreamy mind and that mind's preoccupations, and returning to
the poet's inside reading of the still-life drama that goes on
forever within its frame hanging on the classroom wall.

The ways in which Frost's poem "Stopping by Woods on a
Snowy Evening" converses with Longfellow's translation of
Dante are evident from other shared echoes and images. The
Inferno continues:

> I cannot well repeat how there I entered,
>   So full was I of slumber at the moment
>   In which I had abandoned the true way.
> But after I had reached a mountain's foot,
>   At that point where the valley terminated,
>   Which had with consternation pierced my heart,
> Upward I looked, and I beheld its shoulders,
>   Vested already with that planet's rays
>   Which leadeth others right by every road.
> Then was the fear a little quieted
>   That in my heart's lake had endured throughout
>   That night, which I had passed so piteously.[16]

What Frost "fetched" here (as in "The Road Not Taken") were
the motifs of risk and decision characterizing both "The Choice
of the Two Paths" and Dante's *Inferno*.

"The Draft Horse," a poem published at the end of Frost's life
in his final volume, *In the Clearing* (1962), reminds us curiously

of Frost's anecdote in 1912 about recognizing "another" self and not encountering that self and also of the poem "Stopping by Woods on a Snowy Evening." In addition it is reminiscent of "The Road Not Taken." In each case—anecdote, autumnal poem, and winter poem—the poet must make a choice. Will he "go forward to the touch," or will he "stand still in wonderment and let him pass by" in the anecdote? He will choose the "road less traveled by" (but he will leave the other for a later passing, though he probably will not return to it). He will not succumb to the aesthetic (and perhaps psychological) attractions of the woods, which are "lovely, dark and deep," but will go forth to keep his promises—of both kinds (as Frost explained): "those that I myself make for myself and those that my ancestors made for me, known as the social contract."[17]

> With a lantern that wouldn't burn
> In too frail a buggy we drove
> Behind too heavy a horse
> Through a pitch-dark limitless grove.
>
> And a man came out of the trees
> And took our horse by the head
> And reaching back to his ribs
> Deliberately stabbed him dead.
>
> The ponderous beast went down
> With a crack of a broken shaft.
> And the night drew through the trees
> In one long invidious draft.
>
> The most unquestioning pair
> That ever accepted fate
> And the least disposed to ascribe
> Any more than we had to to hate,
>
> We assumed that the man himself
> Or someone he had to obey
> Wanted us to get down
> And walk the rest of the way.[18]

The "little horse" of the earlier poem is replaced by "the too-heavy horse" of the later one. The "woods" have now been replaced by "a pitch-dark limitless grove." The hint in "grove" is one of sacrificial rites and ordered violence. The "sweep of easy wind and downy flake" of "Stopping by Woods" is echoed more ominously in "The Draft Horse" in that after "the ponderous beast went down" "the night drew through the trees / In one long invidious draft." The man was alone; here he is part of an "unquestioning pair." "Stopping by Woods" was given in the first person. "The Draft Horse," like the beginning of the *Inferno*, takes place in the past. There is resolution in the former—even if it evinces some fatigue; in the latter there is resignation. At the time of the poem and in an earlier day, the loss of a man's horse may be as great a loss as that of one's life—probably because its loss would often lead to the death of the horse's owner. And for the poet the assassination has no rhyme or reason that he will discern. He knows only that the man "came out of the trees" (compare the intruders in "Two Tramps in Mud Time" or the neighbor in "Mending Wall" who resembles "an old-stone savage armed"). Insofar as the poet knows, this act involves motiveless malevolence less than unmalevolent motive—if there is a motive. In the *Inferno*, the beast that threatens the poet's pathway gives way to the poet—"Not man; man once I was," he says—who will guide him. Frost's couple have the misfortune to encounter not a guide but an assassin. "A man feared that he might find an assassin; / Another that he might find a victim," wrote Stephen Crane. "One was more wise than the other."[19] It is not too far-fetched, I think, to see the equanimity of the poet at the end of "The Draft Horse" as a response to the anecdote, many years earlier, when the poet avoided meeting his "other" self, thereby committing the "fatal omission" of not trying to find out what "purpose . . . if we could but have made out" there was in the near-encounter. It is chilling to read the poem against its Frostian antecedents. Yet, as Keeper prefers in *A Masque of Mercy* (1947)—in words out of another context which might better fit the romantic poet of "The Wood-Pile"—"I say I'd rather be lost in the woods / Than found in church."[20]

PART TWO

The Thorosian Poem

SIX

Education by Metaphor

Tell all the Truth but tell it slant—
Success in Circuit lies.
—Emily Dickinson (ca. 1868)

WHEN AMHERST COLLEGE presented Frost with his twenty-first honorary degree in 1948, the poet was cited for having "taught generations of Amherst students that for gaining an insight into life, a metaphor is a sharper and brighter instrument than a syllogism."[1] This remark was meant to characterize the poet as well as the teacher that Frost, try as he might, could never cease to be. But the same comment could have been made, and undoubtedly was made in some form or other, about other native poets: Emerson, for one, whose work, especially his finest essays and lectures, overwhelmed its audience by metaphor and image but spurned ordinary logic; and for another, Thoreau, who chose to argue and persuade not by line and number but through wordplay, narrative, and parable.

The last of these terms—parable—has been applied to Frost as well as to Thoreau. Reginald L. Cook's paper read at the Thoreau centennial meetings in New York City in 1962 usefully distinguishes between Frost and Thoreau as complementary "parablists" while linking them in their devotion to making the parable an effective, and liberating, form for poetic expression.[2] If Frost never publicly defined his own relationship to Thoreau in quite the same way, he left behind enough evidence to convince us that this view of their affinity, as far as it goes, is not off the mark. "I prefer my essay in narrative form," he wrote once. "In *Walden* I get it and always near the height of poetry."[3] As he told Elizabeth Shepley Sergeant, with him Thoreau was "a passion."[4]

Frost's feeling for *Walden* did not diminish through the years. An early strong affection is apparent in Lawrance Thompson's selection of Frost's letters,[5] and the depth of his commitment to Thoreau is made clear in an interview with Reginald Cook, taped for the British Broadcasting Corporation in 1954.[6] In his last college lecture at Dartmouth, delivered scarcely two months before his death, Frost took as his theme the idea of "extravagance," the substance of a striking paragraph at the conclusion of *Walden*—and he did so, moreover, without feeling the need to mention Thoreau at all.[7]

Frost once complained that some recent books of prose could have been written in verse and observed that perhaps they should have been. Still, he took pains to prevent any possible misunderstanding by his correspondent, for he went on to make his point clearly and, in so doing, to acknowledge a pervasive debt to *Walden*: "Far be it from me though to regret that all the poetry isn't in verse. I'm sure I'm glad of all the unversified poetry of Walden—and not merely nature-descriptive, but narrative as in the chapter on the play with the loon on the lake, and character-descriptive as in the beautiful passage about the French-Canadian woodchopper. That last alone with some things in Turgenieff must have had a good deal to do with the making of me."[8] Frost's letter is dated July 15, 1915. He may even then have been thinking about writing the poem that shows the most literal effect of Thoreau's "beautiful passage" about the woodchopper—a poem he was "shaping," apparently, the following spring. For an interview in 1916 quotes him: "Love, the moon, and murder have poetry in them by common consent. But it's in other places. It's in the axe-handle of a French Canadian woodchopper. . . . You know the Canadian woodchoppers whittle their axe-handles, following the curve of the grain, and they're strong and beautiful. Art should follow lines in nature, like the grain of an axe-handle. False art puts curves on things that haven't any curves."[9]

The resemblances between *Walden* and Frost's poem "The Ax-Helve" are pervasive. They include fundamental parallels in the characterizations of Thoreau's woodchopper—whose "so suitable and poetic a name" made the author sorry he could not "print it," Thoreau tells us[10]—and Baptiste, Frost's own French-

Canadian woodsman, who is looking for what the poet calls his "human rating."[11] Baptiste's taut pride in his woodsman's skill has its analogue in *Walden*: "He was a skilful chopper, and indulged in some flourishes and ornaments in his art. He cut his trees level and close to the ground, that the sprouts which came up afterward might be more vigorous and a sled might slide over the stumps; and instead of leaving a whole tree to support his corded wood, he would pare it away to a slender stake or splinter which you could break off with your hand at last" (146). Baptiste, as Frost makes explicit, had a talent for knowing "how to make a short job long / For love of it, and yet not waste time either."[12] So did Thoreau, who tells us he "made no haste in [his] work, but rather made the most of it" (42). And if Baptiste worries that his wife "ain't spick too much Henglish," Thoreau, with no attempt at reproducing the dialect of *his* French-Canadian, reports that his woodsman "considers the best thing he can do in this world," besides maintaining his French, is "to keep up and add to his English" (106).

Such parallels, though substantial, are, after all, elementary, and as such far less telling than the deeper affinities between the two works. Baptiste's adherence to "the curves of his ax-helves" and his faith in the "native . . . grain" recall Thoreau's similar insistence, after making his purchase of old boards, upon "spreading the boards on the grass . . . to bleach and warp back again in the sun" (44). And Frost's ultimate insistence that the good helve is, as a metaphor, contrasted with "laid-on education" may be related to Thoreau's observation that his woodsman's formal instruction has been severely inadequate. Yet if the complaint of Frost's woodchopper against the compulsory "laid-on" education (like the first helve, "made on machine") that works against his natural right to keep his children from school, has behind it a larger question—the question of "whether the right to hold / Such doubts of education should depend / Upon the education of those who held them?"—in *Walden*, Thoreau, attracted to the romantic innocence and natural goodness of his "Homeric" man, is much concerned about the *way* he has been taught: the "innocent and ineffectual way in which the Catholic priests teach the aborigines, by which the pupil is never educated to the degree of consciousness, but only to the degree of trust and reverence, and a child is not made a man, but kept a child" (147).

Thoreau continues his complaint against his woodsman: "I never, by any manoeuvring, could get him to take the spiritual view of things," he writes: "the highest that he appeared to conceive of was a simple expediency, such as you might expect an animal to appreciate. . . . his thinking was so primitive and immersed in his animal life, that, though more promising than a merely learned man's, it rarely ripened to any thing which can be reported" (150). Yet Thoreau, sometimes transcending these strictures at least momentarily, does detect something of importance in his visitor: "There was a certain positive originality, however slight, to be detected in him, and I occasionally observed that he was thinking for himself and expressing his own opinion, a phenomenon so rare that I would any day walk ten miles to observe it, and it amounted to the re-origination of many of the institutions of society. . . . He could defend many institutions better than any philosopher, because, in describing them as they concerned him, he gave the true reason for their prevalence, and speculation had not suggested to him any other" (150,149).

If Thoreau sometimes wondered whether his woodsman "was as wise as Shakespeare or as simply ignorant as a child, whether to suspect him of a fine poetic consciousness or of stupidity" (148), he knew the answer well enough: "In him the animal man chiefly was developed. . . . the intellectual and what is called spiritual man in him were slumbering as in an infant" (146-47). Thoreau's major concern in *Walden* is the development of the spiritual man, but in "Visitors" he addresses himself specifically to the question of such growth through education.

Frost's poem has notably little to do with the Baptiste's skill as a woodsman per se. It does have a great deal to do with "knowledge" and with Baptiste's opinions on education, matters inherent in the analogy that the speaker makes in relation to the perfectly "expressed" ax helve. The apparent strength and willful curves of this helve explicitly recall, compressed into metaphor, the "snake [that] stood up for evil in the Garden." It is as if Frost, seeming to espouse pastoral values and natural forms, has had to express with honesty the "grain" of his own metaphor. Sympathetic as Thoreau was to his natural man of "strong body and contentment" (147), all attempts "to suggest a substitute within him for the priest without, and some higher motive for living" (149) were failures. His natural philosopher remained something of a natural, ready to "live out his three-score years and ten a child" (147). In a sense, so must Frost's French-Canadian, Baptiste, remain an outward priest of nature and an unselfconscious prophet, unwittingly reminding the poet of the "natural" and "innocent" pastoralism of the Garden.

Ultimately both Frost's poem and *Walden* confront the romantic idea that natural man is an embodiment of virtue. That Frost's Baptiste and Thoreau's woodchopper are themselves unaware of the implications of the serpent in Eden (Thoreau, of course, does not emphasize this aspect of the myth) reaffirms the idea that men of undeveloped spirit endanger human culture and the fostering of its values.

Yet if *Walden* does not dwell on the "evils" of natural men, Thoreau does find that the nature of his society compels him to redefine "economy" in humanistic terms, before he can begin to make matter say spirit. Thoreau's basic complaint against society reappears in "The Ax-Helve," more narrowly focused, perhaps, but not more sharply expressed, for the shape of the poet's jerry-built ax helve, two strokes across it, is both serpentine and "economic." *Artificially* crooked, this helve, scorned by Baptiste, who prefers second-growth hickory that "grow[s] crooked," is in a sense the *true* product and the *natural* expression, not of the wood from which it is made, but of the machine which cuts it.[13]

In "House-Warming," on the other hand, Thoreau complains about a different machine: "a small cooking-stove," acquired for the sake of economy, but which "did not keep fire so well as the open fire-place . . . , [for] the stove not only took up room and scented the house, but it concealed the fire" (254). Underlying this observation is Thoreau's vigorous protest in "Economy" against all forms of overheating, particularly overheating through clothing and housing. Thoreau calls attention to the effects of external, physical heat acting upon the inner fire, vital heat, of spirit, fostering torpor as a consequence and injuring the creativity of a man who has work to do. As always, Thoreau's ultimate plea is for the periodic return to those natural, unaccommodated beginnings that are essential to personal growth and spiritual renewal.

The excess of heat at Baptiste's house, an "over-warmth of kitchen stove," like the host's "overjoy," disconcerts the poet. He toys with the idea that the stove endangers Baptiste's wife:

> Mrs. Baptiste came in and rocked a chair
> That had as many motions as the world:
> One back and forward, in and out of shadow,
> That got her nowhere; one more gradual,
> Sideways, that would have run her on the stove[.]

When seen cosmically *and* comically, the rocking of Mrs. Baptiste is a fitting analogue for the motion of the world. The earth's movement, seen in this way—a "rocking" in and out of shadow, in danger of destruction through sideways, crablike slipping into the sun—contains its own principle of self-correction. If the earth seems to right itself periodically, so too does the wife: parodying such physics, she too "realized her danger / And caught herself up bodily, chair and all, / And set herself back where she started from," away from the danger of "over-warmth."

Such motions, "one back and forward" and "one more gradual, / Sideways," interpreted for us by the poet as analogy, are more relevant to those themes of knowledge and education that Baptiste brings up seemingly out of nowhere than may at first appear. The poet watches Baptiste's handling of the ax helve:

> He chafed its long white body
> From end to end with his rough hand shut round it.
> He tried it at the eye-hole in the ax-head.

While Baptiste—in an act deliberately described in sensuous terms—"chafe[s]" the "long white body" of the helve, they talk.

> Do you know, what we talked about was knowledge?
> Baptiste on his defense about the children
> He kept from school, or did his best to keep—
> Whatever school and children and our doubts

> Of laid-on education had to do
> With the curves of his ax-helves. . . .

Whereupon the poet is made to wonder if *he* must decide (in lines previously quoted) "whether the right to hold / Such doubts of education should depend / Upon the education of those who held them." Baptiste's views on education are not entirely alien to those of Frost at this time ("our" doubts, the poet says). Note, for example, the emphasis of his remarks to his friend Sidney Cox in 1915, the year preceding Frost's Phi Beta Kappa reading of "The Ax-Helve" at Harvard:

School is for boning and not for luxuriating. We don't want much school even when we are young, that is to say, we want a great deal more of life than of school. And there is no use in this attempt to make school an image of life. It should be thought of as a thing that belongs to the alphabet and notation. It came into life with these. Life must be kept up at a great rate in order to absorb any considerable amount of either one or the other. Both are nonsense unless they mix well with experience. . . . Too much time spent on them is either an injury to the infant or a waste of time on the infant that refuses to be injured.[14]

Still, Frost's personal view on education is not wholly consonant with that of his rude woodchopper, either.

Consequently, as with the machine that spews out ax helves, *false* education attempts to impose form from without, thereby ignoring the primal grain. Baptiste's simple proposition may be restated: as with good hickory, so with French-Canadian children. His implicit analogy is a reminder that "laid-on education," undermining letter and spirit and violating the root meaning of the word, denies the concept which sees education as "bringing out," "bringing forth." If the values are Thoreau's, they are also those of Emerson, who spoke of the artist's attendance upon form within the "conscious" stone, and who, in the flush of his momentous commitment to nature, it may be recalled, warned man from the book, the lamp, and the library.

But in this poem it is the emerging shape, the "long white body" of the true helve, that counts. Watching Baptiste brush "the shavings from his knee" and watching him stand the ax "on its horse's hoof. / Erect," the poet perceives the analogy to the moment "when / The snake stood up for evil in the Garden." Myth has it that knowledge for Adam and Eve came through knowledge of good and evil; this poem seems to say that Baptiste's art is also knowledge but knowledge that, significantly, is in itself evil *and* good. Perhaps in this section of the poem Frost owes something else to *Walden*. The resemblance to Thoreau's parable of the artist of Kouroo has been recognized by others, but the matter is put concisely, and in the most useful context, by Charles R. Anderson, writing at the time of Frost's death.

Knowledge is the basis of the human condition. Without it man would still be a babe in the Eden woods. With it he is a worker wielding his axe in the clearing, better still an artist shaping forms. This central metaphor, together with the first line of the concluding stanza ("now he brushed the shavings from his knee"), recalls for the reader familiar with "Walden" . . . the fable [of the artist] of Kouroo, who devoted his life to carving a perfect staff only to discover that in the process he had gained immortality. The final worry expressed by God when Adam threatened to turn creator was just that: "lest he put forth his hand, and take also of the tree of life, and eat, and live forever." The danger of a concomitant pride the First Creator well knew from personal experience, as the early verses of Genesis reiterate: "And God saw everything that he had made, and, behold, it was very good." So with Baptiste as he surveys his finished creation: "See how she's cock her head."[15]

Undoubtedly Frost is both wary of and drawn to Eden, to natural innocence and the innocence of nature. Such doubleness is also crucial to Thoreau, who writes in "Higher Laws": "I found in myself, and still find, an instinct toward a higher, or, as it is named, spiritual life, as do most men, and another toward a primitive rank and savage one, and I reverence them both" (210). Nor is the force of this admission diminished when a few paragraphs later Thoreau admits: "We are conscious of an animal in us, which awakens in proportion as our higher nature slumbers. It is reptile and sensual, and perhaps cannot be wholly expelled; like the worms which, even in life and health, occupy our bodies" (219). Thoreau's recognition of the animal in man ("reptile and sensual") corresponds to Frost's perception of the "Edenic" moment, the poet's encounter with the great "Adversary" in the midst of "natural" wisdom and "good" organic form.

Yet it must be noted that, in a romantic sense, the snake in Eden may also represent human consciousness and, implicitly, the possibility of man's spiritual *development*. As such, then, the analogy is a reminder to the poet that even in its snake shape Baptiste's ax helve is good. The serpent as a traditional image of healing—in the caduceus, for example—contradicts the serpentine dollar sign of the poet's first ax helve.

But Frost as craftsman knows that for *this* poem "good and evil" could be too weighty a topic and consequently attempts to make light of it, just as Baptiste's "thick hand" makes "light" of the ax, "top-heavy" with "heaviness." And as in Baptiste's case, physical grace is matched by surprising verbal prowess; the "heaviness" of "good and evil" is handled dextrously with a pleased, mildly sinister observation: "See how she's cock her head!" Unlike his wife, who says nothing at all, Baptiste, like the poet but without his knowledge, anneals word to gesture and in so doing manages to evoke matter and substance far beyond his comprehension.

Frost once admitted that he was a *realist* in poetry if the term meant "one who before all else wants the story to sound as if it were told the way it is because it happened that way." "Of course the story must release an idea," he was quick to caution, "but that is a matter of touch and emphasis, the almost incredible freedom of the soul enslaved to the hard facts of experience."[16] "The Ax-Helve," the poem that deals with shaped and machine-made ax helves, natural knowledge, and "laid-on" education, good and evil, art and commodity, conveys the "realist's" sense of the natural curve in a dramatic situation. But it also illustrates Frost's own successful practice—a practice defined in an exhortation to all poets: "See how figurative you can make a thing *beyond* the figure that is in it."[17] After all, regardless of how it might be out there in the universe, human design in all art *is* of the essence, though his peculiar way, as he claimed, was "twisted"—"with the words cocked a little from the straight out, a little curved from the straight."[18]

SEVEN

Bonfires

> I was present at the auction of a deacon's effects. . . . after lying half a century in his garret and other dust holes, these things were not burned; instead of a *bonfire*, or purifying destruction of them, there was an *auction*, or increasing of them.
> —Henry David Thoreau, *Walden* (1854)

"EVERY MAN LOOKS at his wood-pile with a kind of affection," writes Thoreau in *Walden*.[1] An abandoned wood-pile might evoke other feelings and lead to different thoughts. Hawthorne, for example, has Miles Coverdale, the poet who narrates *The Blithedale Romance*, react in this way:

In my haste, I stumbled over a heap of logs and sticks that had been cut for firewood, a great while ago, by some former possessor of the soil, and piled up square, in order to be carted or sledded away to the farm-house. But, being forgotten, they had lain there, perhaps fifty years, and possibly much longer; until, by the accumulation of moss, and the leaves falling over them and decaying there, from autumn to autumn, a green mound was formed, in which the softened outline of the wood-pile was still perceptible. In the fitful mood that then swayed my mind, I found something strangely affecting in this simple circumstance. I imagined the long-dead woodman, and his long-dead wife and children, coming out of their chill graves, and essaying to make a fire with this heap of mossy fuel![2]

Coverdale's fancy turns toward the uncanny picture of the members of the long-dead woodman's resurrected family joining him in trying to turn this pile of decay into fuel for a fire— trying, that is, to redeem the woodman's labor by using what is left of the woodpile in precisely the way that the woodman must have intended it to be used. The imagined scene, characteristically Hawthorne's, derives much of its poignancy and point from the fact that Hawthorne always places a high premium upon the communal value of the hearth and the fire within.[3]

The most famous woodpile in American letters, however, is not Hawthorne's or even Thoreau's but Robert Frost's. "The Wood-Pile" ends with the poet's meditations:

> I thought that only
> Someone who lived in turning to fresh tasks
> Could so forget his handiwork on which
> He spent himself, the labor of his ax,
> And leave it there far from a useful fireplace
> To warm the frozen swamp as best it could
> With the slow smokeless burning of decay.[4]

Echoing the Creator's work—"The heavens declare the glory of God; and the firmament sheweth his handywork" (Psalm 19:1)—this example of man's handiwork, the abandoned woodpile, rests at a great distance from any house, in the frozen swamp where it will be reclaimed by nature: "The wood was gray and the bark warping off it / And the pile somewhat sunken. Clematis / Had wound strings round and round it like a bundle." If Thoreau had noticed that the stumps of wood in his pile would warm him twice—once when he split them and "again when they were on the fire"[5]—the cord of graying maple that Frost comes upon during his walk into the swamp will warm no human being a second time. The wood will work toward "the slow smokeless burning of decay."[6] In nature there exists more than one way to burn things, to break them down to what they once were. The workings of nature around a man's woodpile serve to remind man that his doings are eccentric and excrescent to the indifferent processes of nature.

If the wood stacked up in the abandoned woodpile will not for a second time warm the woodman responsible for cutting it in the first place, it does serve to inspire the poet, warming him, so to speak, to his poet's task. Indeed, this woodpile as the creation of another, earlier, unidentified and unidentifiable man stands, like the spared tuft of flowers of the earlier poem, as the means by which, working apart and alone, the two beings communicate. The woodpile, slow burning, is the spark that links the woodman and the poet. Having turned away from his midwood creation for "fresh tasks" (thus the approving poet will see it), the woodman leaves behind his handiwork, which will not last forever but has lasted long enough to serve emblematically for the romantic poet who would see a sign.[7] Whether the poem that records the poet's sighting is likely to survive longer than the woodpile remains unasked. Be that as it may, the poem "immortalizes" the mortal creation of a craftsman who built carefully, perhaps as much for the sake of the act of building as for its practical end. The decaying pile in this poem signifies in the same way that the "leaping tongue of flame" signifies in "The Tuft of Flowers."[8]

These comments, however, focus only on the parable quality of the poem. But there is something else going on: a drama that takes the poem forty lines to unfold. To be sure, that drama does not deny the poem's parable ending. It does lead us, though, to an understanding of its true place in this romantic poem.

Dramatically, "The Wood-Pile" tells of an adventure that in retrospect proves to have been a quest. Recalling the descriptive-meditative poetry of Wordsworth and Coleridge, Frost speaks leisurely, in a somewhat wayward fashion, of incidents on a gray day's winter walk that he took by himself. As he tells the story, the poet—alert, perceptive, and adventuresome—reaches a place (or moment) in his walk in the frozen swamp when he must decide whether to turn back or go further. He will go further: "and we shall see"—he tells himself. "See" means, as it turns out, what the poet shall notice, what he will perceive. He notices that the snow is hard but that "now and then" his foot breaks through the crust. "Tall slim trees," all in lines, "straight up and down," look too much alike for him to "mark or name a place by" them. In short, he's not sure whether he is "here / Or somewhere else." Willy-nilly, he puts into practice his own later advice (echoing Thoreau) that you must be "lost enough to find yourself."[9] So far Frost knows merely that he is "just far from home." A small bird passes. The poet, taking careful notice, begins to attribute attitudes and motives to the creature who now shares his space. The bird, who says "no word to tell me

who he was," recalls no Coleridgian nightingale. The poet sees
the bird as self-centered, fearful (perhaps vain), taking "every-
thing said as personal to himself." Just like the poet himself, one
might observe, a romantic egotist out looking for experience,
any experience, as long as it is suitable for framing an interpre-
tation. The self-centered poet recalls himself in the act of look-
ing for symbols he can take personally. And here he sees "a pile
of wood," for which he forgets the small bird, "without so much
as wishing him good-night." The romantic poet has found his
symbol, for as Thoreau informs us, "after all our discoveries and
inventions no man will go by a pile of wood,"[10] and it turns
out to be nothing more, nothing less, than a New England ruin
like Hawthorne's woodpile. This decaying pile—so unlike
Wordsworth's Peele Castle, that "rugged" and "hoary Pile"
withstanding the "sea in anger"[11]—calls to the poet's mind
sobering thoughts pertaining to the nature and fate of man's
handiwork.

In taking everything personally, then, the poet has a dual
experience: he renews his perception that man (including him-
self) is a small thing within nature, and, as the self-serving poet,
he reaches his goal, redeems his somewhat aimless walk, and
finds the culminating symbol necessary and sufficient for his
romantic's poem. What the return walk brought him he does not
tell us. The boon this hero has brought back from his journey is
no more, we surmise, than the poem of winter (snow), bird (no
nightingale, no skylark, no raven), and ruins—all of them em-
blematic of a rather plain world.

But "The Wood-Pile" also stands as an oblique paean to
craftsmanship and, if you will, to art and poetry. The maker of
this woodpile, according to the writer of the poem, lives in the
work he has left behind: "a cord of maple, cut and split / And
piled—measured, four by four by eight," held on one side by "a
tree" and on the other by "a stake and prop"—the former "still
growing," the latter "about to fall." In short, the woodpile
results from the exercise of craft. It is not even known for certain
that the split wood was intended for anything beyond his wood-
pile, though common sense rejects the possibility that the mak-
ing of the woodpile was the woodman's sole end. That the
crafted pile decays, breaking down to its elements, says much

about the impermanence of man's handiwork—a point which brings us back to man's continuing quiet astonishment at the transformation of all his work—the noble and the banal—into waste and ruin.

Then there are the fires we call fire. "That spring bonfire," for example, "with its smells to recur for a lifetime to come, was fun for all the family. But one of those bonfires nearly turned into a catastrophe. In answer to a query, he replied, 'Yes, Derry was where I got the scare about a grass fire.' "[12] Of the two poems Frost read before the Phi Beta Kappa Society at Harvard University in 1916 ("The Ax-Helve" and "The Bonfire"), neither of them, as he had written to Louis Untermeyer shortly before the reading, could be called "either timely or appropriate"—a shared feature in their favor, he insisted, for "one is old old and the other is new and so older than the first because it was written by an older man."[13] After the reading, Frost reported that the editor of the *Atlantic Monthly* (Ellery Sedgwick) had liked the poem with "the Frenchman in it" but had not liked "The Bonfire."[14]

Despite Frost's letter to Untermeyer before the reading, however, "The Bonfire" was intended to be timely. It was, at least in part, a war poem. Although it was written years earlier (the fire that had so scared him took place in April 1905) he had apparently brought the poem up to date, so to speak, for he incorporated, according to his biographer, "internal references to zeppelin bombings of England in World War One."[15] Unfortunately, Frost is not entirely successful in the attempt to achieve an aesthetically meaningful topicality. One can say with sureness that he, almost shamefully, tries to "fetch" the war into his early poem.

Frost tries to impose a topical meaning on the central (and initial) experience of the poem: the fires retrospectively and prospectively seen. The unstoppable fire is capable of enormous destruction, and such a conflagration reminds him of war and of what it can do. The Great War, in 1915, was of course already under way. And what more timely topic for Harvard's young Phi Beta Kappans, what more up-to-the-moment theme, could there be than the war in Europe? But the comparison is too easy—the "war" that a fire wages against everything in its way and the "fire" that is a war, consuming men, destroying material, and ravaging nature itself. Frost does little apart from linking fire and war. He admitted as much when, a couple of years later, he confessed that "The Bonfire" was "more of New England than of what is going on over yonder."[16] No, what is salvageable in the poem occurs before the poet slips into the obvious comparison. The apocalyptic poet who found that there was no choosing between destruction by fire and destruction by ice finds that the fire, set in the spring to burn away aftermath, has, when it burns its way uncomfortably beyond the barriers created by human beings, a second benefit. Besides burning over land that will serve for pasture or some sort of planting, it provides the farmer who set the fire with an opportunity for exhilaration and fear—man's primitive feelings before the elemental force of fire. Here is something akin to Emerson's feeling, while crossing "a bare common": "Almost I fear to think how glad I am."[17] To start a fire, to control its burning, to lose that control, and then—in the midst of great fear—to reestablish it, is a prospect not unattractive to the poet, who, remembering such a fire, is ready to start a new one.

The bonfire of the poem's title refers to the several "fires" in the poem. It is both the fire that the narrator remembers and the fire he is urging others to join him in setting. And it is the fire that is war and which at the time of the poem's reading at Harvard was already raging in Europe. Are these all "bon" fires, that is to say, "good" fires, that will bring about, in Thoreau's terms, a "purifying destruction"?[18] Are such fires necessary for the renewal of races, individual lives, vegetation, nations, and peoples? Moreover, do these fires presage an apocalyptic fire that will destroy the world? Frost's runaway fire (and the fear attending it as well as the pleasure taken in the controlling of it) has given him a sense of the apocalypse: starting a fire, fearing it, and controlling it—being nicked once by the apocalypse but escaping it to try again.

He escapes it, in fact, as an artist will touch on calamity and destruction within the danger (and safety) inherent to his own métier. The earth is his canvas—or at least a small piece of it. Fire is instrumental to his craft. His is a "vulcanic" art that *changes* the world, transforms its color. Walter Pater had advocated living for moments that burn with a hard, gemlike flame. His ethical imperative was to experience as many of those moments as possible. It is as if, in "The Bonfire," Frost had turned the search for moments burning with a clear, gemlike flame into the unleashing of a runaway fire, a conflagration that wildly spreads its "coal-black" color over ten times the area anyone else ever did in the time it took him to do it. It is as if Frost were answering the Emerson who wrote of nature:

To the attentive eye, each moment of the year has its own beauty, and in the same field, it beholds, every hour, a picture which was never seen before, and which shall never be seen again. The heavens change every moment, and reflect their glory or gloom on the plains beneath. The state of the crop in the surrounding farms alters the expression of the earth from week to week. The succession of native plants in the pastures and road-sides, which make the silent clock by which time tells the summer hours, will make even the divisions of the day sensible to a keen observer. The tribes of birds and insects, like the plants punctual to their time, follow each other, and the year has room for all. By watercourses, the variety is greater. In July, the blue pontederia or pickerelweed blooms in large beds in the shallow parts of our pleasant river, and swarms with yellow butterflies in continual motion. Art cannot rival this pomp of purple and gold.[19]

Perhaps, but Frost the fire-painter has his own claim: "But I'm sure no one ever spread / Another color over a tenth the space / That I spread coal-black over in the time / It took me."[20]

Frost's fire brings out in him pleasure analogous to that of Emerson on the bare common. It is as if the poet has "said" fire and there is fire. He expresses the power, not of the benevolent Creator, but of the demonic demiurge. His own experience licenses him to speak with stern and authoritative prophecy in "Fire and Ice."

> Some say the world will end in fire,
> Some say in ice.
> From what I've tasted of desire
> I hold with those who favor fire.
> But if it had to perish twice,
> I think I know enough of hate

To say that for destruction ice
Is also great
And would suffice.[21]

Those who prophesied that the world might end in ice included Henry David Thoreau. In "House-Warming" (*Walden*) Thoreau insists that we need not "trouble ourselves to speculate how the human race may be at last destroyed." For, as he argues, "It would be easy to cut their threads any time with a little sharper blast from the north. We go on dating from Cold Fridays and Great Snows; but a little colder Friday, or greater snow, would put a period to man's existence on the globe."[22] Thoreau's remarks are embedded in the final paragraphs of the chapter, which are devoted to fire and smoke and physical warmth. Frost does not, of course, take over Thoreau directly. Rather he will trouble himself to think about man's demise. If the human race might be destroyed by ice (or by fire), the human apocalypse might well come about, in the poet's analogies, through hatred (or through love). As with the elements, so, it would seem, with the emotions. "That row of icicles along the gutter," writes the poet in "Beyond Words," "Feels like my armory of hate."[23]

Frost's mock-heroic treatment of the theme of "fire and ice" focusing on the diurnal and seasonal rhythms of heat and cold carries the title "A Hillside Thaw." Superficially playful, the poem fetches words, images, and situation from Thoreau. In "Spring" (*Walden*) Thoreau writes:

At length the sun's rays have attained the right angle, and warm winds blow up mist and rain and melt the snow banks. . . . Few phenomena give me more delight than to observe the forms which thawing sand and clay assume in flowing down the sides of a deep cut on the railroad. . . . When the frost comes out in the spring, and even in a thawing day in the winter, the sand begins to flow down the slopes like lava, sometimes bursting out through the snow and overflowing it where no sand was to be seen before. . . . As it flows it takes the forms of sappy leaves or vines, making heaps of pulpy sprays a foot or more in depth, and resembling, as you look down on them, the laciniated lobed and imbricated thalluses of some lichens; or you are reminded of coral, of leopards' paws or birds' feet, of brains or lungs or bowels, and excrements of all kinds. . . . When the sun withdraws the sand ceases to flow, but in the morning the streams will start once more and branch and branch again into a myriad of others. . . . from the thawing mass . . . is seen a little silvery stream glancing like lightning from one stage of pulpy leaves or branches to another, and ever and anon swallowed up in the sand. . . . Ere long, not only on these banks, but on every hill and plain and every hollow, the frost comes out of the ground like a dormant quadruped from its burrow, and seeks the sea with music, or migrates to other climes in clouds. Thaw with his gentle persuasion is more powerful than Thor with his hammer. The one melts, the other but breaks in pieces.[24]

In the forms taken by the flowing thaw in his poem, Frost sees not Thoreau's imagery of brains or lungs or coral or even birds' feet or leopards' paws. He sees lizards—silver lizards (Thoreau's "silvery stream[s]"). And when he describes the thaw as it takes place in the warm sunlight, he does so to tell you about his own inability to capture or fix even one of these members of a "wet stampede." The unpleasantness of these "silver lizards" is conveyed unmistakably in the poet's observation that in their "wriggling" the "ten million silver lizards out of the snow" look to him "as if some magic of the sun / Lifted the rug that bred them on the floor / And the light breaking on them made them run."[25]

These Thoreauvian qualities are attended to in the first half of "A Hillside Thaw," but the second half of the poem swerves well away from Thoreau's remarks in *Walden*. While Thoreau merely acknowledges the passing of sunlight and the effect of its passing on the thaw ("when the sun withdraws the sand ceases to flow, but in the morning"), Frost focuses on the loss of heat as it affects the thaw, choosing to attribute this effect to the moon, "a witch," even as the sun is "a wizard."

> It takes the moon for this. The sun's a wizard
> By all I tell; but so's the moon a witch.
> From the high west she makes a gentle cast
> And suddenly, without a jerk or twitch,
> She has her spell on every single lizard.
> I fancied when I looked at six o'clock
> The swarm still ran and scuttled just as fast.
> The moon was waiting for her chill effect.
> I looked at nine: the swarm was turned to rock

In every lifelike posture of the swarm,
Transfixed on mountain slopes almost erect.
Across each other and side by side they lay.
The spell that so could hold them as they were
Was wrought through trees without a breath of storm
To make a leaf, if there had been one, stir.
It was the moon's: she held them until day.
One lizard at the end of every ray.
The thought of my attempting such a stay!

The moon is obviously working its poetry, creating a momentary (say nightlong) stay against confusion (the leaping lizards, ten million of them). But the moon has also given one possible answer to the question Thoreau has earlier avoided: that we need not "trouble ourselves to speculate how the human race may be at last destroyed." Let the world end in ice. Will that not be an answer to life's confusions and wearying "considerations"?

EIGHT

Economy

> We will know the meaning of our economies and politics.
> —Ralph Waldo Emerson, "Uses of Great Men" (1876)

"TWO TRAMPS IN MUD TIME" was first published in 1934. At the time Frost remarked that he considered the poem to be "against having hobbies."[1] Two years later, when he collected it in *A Further Range* as one of ten poems to be "taken doubly," he added to its title in the list of contents the thematic phrase, "*or, A Full-Time Interest.*" In both instances Frost provided a clue to his intended meaning. Unfortunately, critical interpretations of the poem have seldom pursued the leads suggested by the poet.

Two such commentaries, published twenty years apart, are particularly instructive regarding the manner in which each reaches out for the meaning of the poem. Each sees the poem as a vehicle for an idea, for a social ideology, but neither finds it necessary to locate the poem in the context of traditional American thought and literature.

Denis Donoghue, writing in 1965, reads "Two Tramps in Mud Time" as a clear instance of the relation between Frost's "temperament and the ideas of Social Darwinism."[2] The poet did not find compelling the arguments for giving the tramps a job, and hence Donoghue reaches this puzzling conclusion: "So need is not reason enough. The narrator has need and love on his side, hence he survives and nature blesses him as the best man. The tramps are unfit to survive because they have only their need, and the Darwinist law is that they should not survive." Donoghue's overall reading of Frost's poem, not to mention his extraordinary application of Darwinist law, defies explanation. The idea that conjoined need and love constitute in themselves a higher claim for survival than need alone is a curious form of Darwinism. Frost's poem does show a concern with personal integrity and the survival of the human spirit, but nowhere does it come close to hinting that need without love, lamentable as it may be, actually renders the mud-time tramps unfit for survival. The narrator may have need and love "on his side" (as Donoghue puts it), but this fact hardly constitutes evidence either that the situation enables him to survive or that "nature blesses him as the best man." There is no indication, either within the confines of the poem or in the facts of the poet's life as we know them, that "Two Tramps in Mud Time" is intended to recall Charles Darwin or to echo the Social Darwinists.

Donoghue's reading bears a curious relationship to Malcolm Cowley's famous commentary on the poem, made more than forty years ago. His Darwinist interpretation is an offshoot of Cowley's "liberal" chastisement of Frost in the *New Republic* in 1944.[3] Donoghue offers a specific reason for Frost's behavior toward the tramps, while Cowley describes and deplores the poet's reaction to their request. But both critics are interested in faulting the poet for his inhumanity. "In spite of his achievements as a narrative and lyric poet," argues the dissenting Cowley, there is "a case against Robert Frost as a social philosopher in verse and as a representative of the New England tradition" of Ralph Waldo Emerson and Henry David Thoreau. Assuming that the poem reflects an actual incident of the depression years, Cowley criticizes Frost for evading the socioeconomic fortune of the masses and retreating into "sermon." Instead of helping men who want work, preaches Cowley, "Frost turns to the reader with a sound but rather sententious sermon on the ethical value of the chopping block."

To acknowledge that Cowley's account of the poem has some, albeit limited, merit, is not, however, to endorse his vestigial reading with its earmarks of the 1930s. It may be granted that Frost was an early outspoken foe of the social excesses he found exhibited in Franklin Delano Roosevelt and the administrators of his New Deal.[4] But to insist unequivocally that in this poem Frost lacks all social conscience is to mislead grievously. Cowley's concept of a social conscience is at best limited.

That the strangers who come at him "out of the mud"[5] display great need, Frost acknowledges. Too readily is his head filled with the narrow logic that he has "no right to play / With what was another man's work for gain." "My right might be love but theirs was need," he admits; "and where the two exist in twain / Theirs was the better right—agreed." Frost is not insensitive to the tramps' need for "gain," for shelter and food perhaps, but, individualist that he is, he is too thoroughly self-reliant and humanistic to assign all priority to satisfying such basic needs. Rather, he hopes to remind us, in offering himself as example, that men have other kinds of need as well and that their failure to meet those needs results from their inability to recognize the high necessity that "love and need" must make one ("as my two eyes make one in sight"). This failure, common to men everywhere, is particularized for the moment in the tramps whose only thought was that, claiming *economic* need, "all chopping was theirs of right." Frost deplores, of course, the plight of the unfortunates who for whatever reason must totally dissociate need and love, vocation and avocation. He does not deny that poverty is problematic to society, but he does indicate that the necessity for any man to work much or all of his time for pay alone will rapidly dissolve his sense of other values of self and spirit. He concludes triumphantly:

> Only where love and need are one,
> And the work is play for mortal stakes,
> Is the deed ever really done
> For Heaven and the future's sakes.

Frost's ideology in this poem has its roots deep in the nineteenth century, and to understand his poem's relationship to that century, we must turn, *pace* Donoghue and Cowley, to the traditions of Concord transcendentalism. Specifically, we must look to Henry Thoreau, whose work, encountered early, had a pervasive and formative impact on Frost's life as well as on his poetry. The spiritual morality of the individual self expressed in "Two Tramps" is endemic to both Thoreau and Frost, while Frost's economy accords perfectly with Thoreau's views on work and labor as nurture for the human spirit. In "Two

Tramps" the kinship of Frost and Thoreau is evident at every turn.

Take *Walden* for the moment. In chapter 13 Thoreau contemplates his metaphoric "House-Warming." He begins by talking about woodpiles:

I loved to have mine before my window, and the more chips the better to remind me of my pleasing work. I had an old axe which nobody claimed, with which by spells in winter days, on the sunny side of the house, I played about the stumps which I had got out of my bean-field. As my driver prophesied when I was plowing, they warmed me twice, once while I was splitting them, and again when they were on the fire, so that no fuel could give out more heat.[6]

These few sentences anticipate Frost's poem as a unit, but they have their closest dramatic equivalence in the second and sixth stanzas:

> Good blocks of oak it was I split,
> As large around as the chopping block;
> And every piece I squarely hit
> Fell splinterless as a cloven rock.[7]
> . . . .
> You'd think I never had felt before
> The weight of an ax-head poised aloft,
> The grip on earth of outspread feet.
> The life of muscles rocking soft
> And smooth and moist in vernal heat.

In situation, motif, and theme, the passage from *Walden* offers a meaningful context for "Two Tramps."

For a full understanding of the transcendental tradition behind Frost's poem, however, a more useful document is Thoreau's brilliant essay "Life without Principle." A discursive presentation of his central ideas on society, labor, and the self, this essay was published in the *Atlantic Monthly* in 1863, after having served for several years as a lyceum talk. It is an important manifestation of Thoreau's dedication to the spiritual needs of the self and to the idea that the self must be served constantly in its struggle against the destructive pressures of

socialization. As such, it can now serve us as a kind of manifesto
of the intellectual and literary tradition to which "Two Tramps
in Mud Time" properly belongs.

Frost is wary of those who want to take his "job for pay."
Thoreau's more generalized complaint makes the same point.
"The ways by which you may get money almost without excep-
tion lead downward. To have done anything by which you
earned money *merely* is to have been truly idle or worse. If the
laborer gets no more than the wages which his employer pays
him, he is cheated, he cheats himself."[8] In fact, such a laborer is
deceived in that he is "paid for being something less than a
man" when his aim should be "not to get his living . . . but to
perform well a certain work. . . . Do not hire a man who does
your work for money," cautions Thoreau, "but him who does it
for love of it."[9]

Frost takes these Thoreauvian ideals and dramatizes them in
his lyric poem. It is not the tramps who work for the love of the
work, it turns out, but the poet himself, and consequently he
cannot without compromise and self-betrayal give way to those
who work merely for wages. He must, in Thoreau's words, "be
fastidious to the extreme of sanity, disregarding the gibes of
those who are more unfortunate than ourselves."[10] Thoreau
reminds us that, surprisingly, "a man may be very industrious,
and yet not spend his time well": "There is no more fatal
blunderer than he who consumes the greater part of his life
getting his living. All great enterprises are self-supporting. The
poet, for instance, must sustain his body by his poetry, as a
steam planing-mill feeds its boilers with the shavings it makes.
You must get your living by loving."[11]

The values that Thoreau conveys discursively and didac-
tically in "Life without Principle" Frost exalts in narrative
subsumed by lyric. Given such commitments, there is no ques-
tion that Frost must fail Cowley's test in socioeconomics and
collectivist philosophy, but so must Thoreau. Frost might have
said, with Thoreau: "To be supported by the charity of friends,
or a government pension,—provided you continue to breathe,—
by whatever fine synonyms you describe these relations, is to go
into the almshouse."[12] Frost did say that a man "should be a
large-proportioned individual before he becomes social."[13]

In sum, "Two Tramps in Mud Time" should not be read as the one-sided, frontal attack on socialist or collectivist thinking that Cowley would have it be, nor should it be read as Donoghue's illustrative apologia for the wondrous workings of Darwinist law. Grounded in social and transcendental ideas the poet shares with Henry Thoreau, the poem stands in opposition to that capacity for self-betrayal and degeneration which inheres in each and every man: that propensity to "quarter our gross bodies on our poor souls, till the former eat up all the latter's substance."[14] When the thematic and ideological affinities of Frost and Thoreau are fully recognized, we shall have a surer sense of what Frost is about in his poem "against having hobbies." Thoreau's statement that "the whole duty of life is contained in the question how to respire and aspire both at once"[15] is an adage the import of which Frost seems not to have missed. As he insisted in the early 1950s, at the age of seventy-eight, "I have never outgrown anything that I ever liked. I have never had a hobby in my life, but I have ranged through a lot of things."[16]

NINE

Smoke

> The whited air hides hills & woods, the river & the heaven
> & veils the farmhouse at the garden's end. The traveller
> stopped & sled the courier's feet delayed all friends shut
> out the housemates sit around the radiant fireplace
> enclosed in a tumultuous privacy of storm.
> —Ralph Waldo Emerson, *Notebooks* (1834)

SAFETY AND COMFORT against the elements is Thoreau's subject in "House-Warming." Toward the end of the chapter he turns to answer those who criticized his decision to move to Walden Pond.

Some of my friends spoke as if I was coming to the woods on purpose to freeze myself. The animal merely makes a bed, which he warms with his body in a sheltered place; but man, having discovered fire, boxes up some air in a spacious apartment, and warms that, instead of robbing himself, makes that his bed, in which he can move about divested of more cumbrous clothing, maintain a kind of summer in the midst of winter, and by means of windows even admit the light, and with a lamp lengthen out the day.[1]

This notion, which is common enough, resurfaces in Frost's long dramatic poem, "Snow":

> The wind's at naught in here.
> It couldn't stir so sensitively poised
> A thing as that. It couldn't reach the lamp
> To get a puff of black smoke from the flame,
> Or blow a rumple in the collie's coat.
> You make a little foursquare block of air,
> Quiet and light and warm, in spite of all
> The illimitable dark and cold and storm. . . .[2]

Within this "foursquare block of air," as Thoreau deliberately and at great length observes, is the fire man makes to warm up that bed of enclosed air, a fire that produces smoke. Thoreau quotes two major poems celebrating the fire and smoke produced by human beings, one of which is his poem beginning "Lightwinged Smoke, Icarian bird" and ending "Go thou my incense upward from this hearth, / And ask the gods to pardon this clear flame."[3] Frost reacted in an interesting way to Thoreau's attitudes toward man-made warmth and man-made smoke. He worked the two Thoreauvian subjects into a sixteen-line poem, "The Cocoon," published in *West-Running Brook* (1928).

> As far as I can see this autumn haze
> That spreading in the evening air both ways,
> Makes the new moon look anything but new,
> And pours the elm-tree meadow full of blue,
> Is all the smoke from one poor house alone
> With but one chimney it can call its own;
> So close it will not light an early light,
> Keeping its life so close and out of sight
> No one for hours has set a foot outdoors
> So much as to take care of evening chores.
> The inmates may be lonely women-folk.
> I want to tell them that with all this smoke
> They prudently are spinning their cocoon
> And anchoring it to an earth and moon
> From which no winter gale can hope to blow it,—
> Spinning their own cocoon did they but know it.[4]

Like the house itself, the smoke sent up from that house is also an enclosure. But significantly this enclosure does not separate the house and those within it from the outside but makes a connection (an anchor, the poet says) to "an earth and moon / From which no winter gale can hope to blow it." This smoke is not incense, as Thoreau would have it, emanating from a "clear flame" that the gods would need to "pardon," but it shapes itself prudently into something protective—a cocoon—that will shield whatever is within that cocoon, larvae or human beings. Still, their need for such protective anchoring makes the inhabi-

tants reluctant to leave the house, even temporarily to do their
chores. This association of smoke from a man-made fire with
human timidity is anticipated in another of Thoreau's remark-
able but neglected poems, "Smoke in Winter."

> The sluggish smoke curls up from some deep dell,
> The stiffened air exploring in the dawn,
> And making slow acquaintance with the day;
> Delaying now upon its heavenward course,
> In wreathed loiterings dallying with itself,
> With as uncertain purpose and slow deed,
> As its half-wakened master by the hearth,
> Whose mind still slumbering and sluggish thoughts
> Have not yet swept into the onward current
> Of the new day;—and now it streams afar,
> The while the chopper goes with step direct,
> And mind intent to swing the early axe.
>   First in the dusky dawn he sends abroad
> His early scout, his emissary, smoke,
> The earliest, latest pilgrim from the roof,
> To feel the frosty air, inform the day;
> And while he crouches still beside the hearth,
> Nor musters courage to unbar the door,
> It has gone down the glen with the light wind,
> And o'er the plain unfurled its venturous wreath,
> Draped the tree tops, loitered upon the hill,
> And warmed the pinions of the early bird;
> And now, perchance, high in the crispy air,
> Has caught sight of the day o'er the earth's edge,
> And greets its master's eye at his low door,
> As some refulgent cloud in the upper sky.[5]

The movement in the poem apes the drifting, curling course of
the smoke emanating from a hearth by which its "half-wakened
master" continues to "crouch," his own "sluggish thoughts"
having not yet been "swept into the onward current / Of the
new day." His mind still slumbers, but the chopper steps di-
rectly, his "mind intent to swing the early axe." Even at the end
of the poem—when the smoke has wafted so far into the air that
it now greets its "master's eye," that eye is still no closer to the

outside than the "low door." The smoke does all the acting—the moving—in this poem, and we cannot be at all certain that the sight of the far-off smoke—like some shining cloud far off high in the sky—will succeed in encouraging the master to "unbar the door" and venture out boldly like the chopper.

In one of Thoreau's earliest poems, which begins with the line "Within the circuit of this plodding life," the poet celebrates the restorative power of memory. The memory of benevolent pictures of spring and summer's experience—of violets, anemones, and meandering rivulets—inspires and invigorates the poet in the midst of frosty nights and winter snows:

> I have remembered when the winter came,
> High in my chamber in the frosty nights,
> When in the still light of the cheerful moon,
> On every twig and rail and jutting spout,
> The icy spears were adding to their length
> Against the arrows of the coming sun,
> How in the shimmering noon of summer past
> Some unrecorded beam slanted across
> The upland pastures where the Johnswort grew;
> Or heard, amid the verdure of my mind,
> The bee's long smothered hum, on the blue flag
> Loitering amidst the mead; or busy rill. . . .
> Or seen the furrows shine but late upturned,
> And where the fieldfare followed in the rear,
> When all the fields around lay bound and hoar
> Beneath a thick integument of snow.
> So by God's cheap economy made rich
> To go upon my winter's task again.[6]

Thoreau's notion of the restorative memory, echoed by Emerson in his poem "The World-Soul,"[7] derives rather directly from the romantic poets, from Wordsworth particuarly, in a poem such as "Lines Composed a Few Miles above Tintern Abbey." It was available to Frost, but in an early poem ("Storm Fear") it is as if the poet had stubbornly refused to avail himself of such memories, or, perhaps more accurately, he had been compelled to behave with the knowledge that for him at least the memory of a summer day is sometimes besides the point.

When the wind works against us in the dark,
And pelts with snow
The lower chamber window on the east,
And whispers with a sort of stifled bark,
The beast,
'Come out! Come out!'—
It costs no inward struggle not to go,
Ah, no!
I count our strength,
Two and a child,
Those of us not asleep subdued to mark
How the cold creeps as the fire dies at length,—
How drifts are piled,
Dooryard and road ungraded,
Till even the comforting barn grows far away,
And my heart owns a doubt
Whether 'tis in us to arise with day
And save ourselves unaided.[8]

Thoreau could end his poem with the acknowledgment that through God's economy the poet was fortified to go upon his winter's task. There is no evidence in Frost's poem that any such example of "God's cheap economy" is forthcoming to support those inside who would avoid the wintery beast calling to them, "Come out! Come out!"

But such doubts, even on balance, are atypical of Frost's bolder humanistic stands. As is made clear in the last poem—untitled—of the final section (entitled "Quandary") of Frost's last book, *In the Clearing*, the poet has little sympathy for those who will not venture out in winter snow to deliver a "blow" against something out there in Nature. He himself behaves differently.

In winter in the woods alone
Against the trees I go.
I mark a maple for my own
And lay the maple low.

At four o'clock I shoulder axe
And in the afterglow

I link a line of shadowy tracks
Across the tinted snow.

I see for Nature no defeat
In one tree's overthrow
Or for myself in my retreat
For yet another blow.[9]

There's no holding back at the "low door," nor for that matter is there any of the sense of senseless and dispiriting routine about Frost's woodman's move "against the trees" that is evident in Thoreau's remarks toward the end of *Walden:* "It is remarkable how easily and insensibly we fall into a particular route, and make a beaten track for ourselves. I had not lived there a week before my feet wore a path from my door to the pond-side; and though it is five or six years since I trod it, it is still quite distinct. It is true, I fear that others may have fallen into it, and so helped to keep it open."[10] No danger here, in Frost's late poem, for the "line of shadowy tracks" he "link[s]" are made over snow. And besides, the task he has set for himself and carried out precludes repetition. No path will be worn between his cabin (or from any other starting point) and the one maple he has marked for his own. It is a one-time job to lay that maple low (as it is to cut down any tree). The path, perhaps never before taken just exactly in the way the chopper has taken it on this day, need never be taken again for the same purpose. There is no possibility here of succumbing to a dispiriting routine.

Yet the connection Thoreau makes between the "sluggish-[ness]" of the man-made smoke and the "sluggish" thoughts in the "still slumbering" mind of the reluctant "master" of the cabin or house is not absent in Frost. In "A Cabin in the Clearing," which also comes from *In the Clearing,* the trepidations of Thoreau's master of the hearth bear a certain resemblance to the attitudes expressed in the dialogue between the personifications of Mist and Smoke in Frost's poem. The question posed by Mist, who doesn't believe that the sleepers within "this house / Know where they are" is answered by Smoke, who sees himself as the would-be protector of those within the cabin: "I am the guardian wraith of starlit smoke / That leans out this and that way from their chimney. / I will not have their happiness despaired of."[11] Unfortunately, they do not know who they are and therefore do not know where they are. Mist doubts that they will ever know where they are, for although (as Smoke observes) they have been around "long enough / To push the woods back from around the house / And part them in the middle with a path," they have maintained that path, according to Mist, for "the comfort / Of visiting with the equally bewildered. / Nearer in plight their neighbors are than distance." Here is an analogue for Thoreau's beaten path from his cabin to the pondside, but it is no analogue for the path in the snow made by Frost's adventuresome chopper. Within the cabin in the clearing, however, as Mist says to Smoke, they seem at first to come into their own.

> They murmur talking in the dark
> On what should be their daylong theme continued.
> Putting the lamp out has not put their thought out.
> Let us pretend the dewdrops from the eaves
> Are you and I eavesdropping on their unrest—
> A mist and smoke eavesdropping on a haze—
> And see if we can tell the bass from the soprano.

In an italicized coda to the sustained dialogue between Mist and Smoke, the poet adds a question that does not end in a question mark: "Than smoke and mist who better could appraise / The kindred spirit of an inner haze." Who better, it is chilling to ask, than the ephemeral smoke and the mist that "cotton[s] to their landscape"? What they will eavesdrop on, though, is nothing less than the sound of sentences—the sound sentences make even when one cannot hear the words. What the Smoke and the Mist will hear will be the "poetry" made by those within the cabin as they continue their "daylong theme" after the lamps (which should have put out their thought) have themselves been put out.

Poetry could not function as a little foursquare block of air that is a house, nor should it. It must never be a cocoon either, one that works beneficially to protect those within from changes outside and detrimentally to insulate those so protected from experience. Yet poetry can be a human construction, even for those still bemused at night by their day-long theme, thrown up as that momentary stay against confusion. Knowing the bass from the soprano is only a little less important than the fact that the bass and soprano exist. "Granted no one but a humanist much cares how sound a poem is if it is only *a* sound," wrote Frost, "[but] the sound is the gold in the ore."[12]

TEN

Solitary Singer

In June the morning is noisy with birds; in August they are already old and silent.
—Ralph Waldo Emerson, "Inspiration" (1872)

IN "THE OVEN BIRD" the poet transposes the creature's midsummer, midwood sound into words: "the highway dust is over all."[1] Indicative of the onset in midsummer New England of seasonal dessication, this image contributes metaphorically to our emotional acquiescence in the larger import of the theme posed in the question he "frames in all but words": "what to make of a diminished thing."

The almost casual reference to "dust," however, links this poem to others in the Frost canon. A look at poems such as "Dust of Snow," "My Butterfly," and "Dust in the Eyes" will usefully precede a fuller consideration of "The Oven Bird."

> The way a crow
> Shook down on me
> The dust of snow
> From a hemlock tree
>
> Has given my heart
> A change of mood
> And saved some part
> Of a day I had rued.[2]

In a fine explication of Frost's "Dust of Snow" (*New Hampshire*, 1923), Laurence Perrine asks and answers the question "Why did he use the word *dust?*" "Because it is visually exact, and because alternative wordings—'powdery snow' or 'feathery snow,' for example—lack the simplicity of meter and diction that he was after."[3] To these reasons I would add another: he was reaching back to one of his own earlier uses of the word *dust*. In "My Butterfly" (1894) he had referred to the butterfly's "dye-dusty wing." The lines in which the phrase occurs bear a certain thematic and situational resemblance to the later poem.

> Ah! I remember me
> How once conspiracy was rife
> Against my life
>   (The languor of it!), and
> Surging, the grasses dizzied me of thought,
> The breeze three odors brought,
>   And a gem flower waved in a wand.
> Then, when I was distraught
>   And could not speak,
>   Sidelong, full on my cheek,
> What should that reckless zephyr fling
> But the wild touch of your dye-dusty wing![4]

The poet goes on to talk of finding, sometime later, that very wing "with the withered leaves / Under the eaves." The connection of these lines with "Dust of Snow," however, does not extend to Frost's naturalistic conclusion in the earlier poem. The connection is that in both instances—the lines quoted above and the poem "Dust of Snow"—the poet is brought out of some state of being that is unpleasant through an unexpected intrusion into his consciousness by a natural event—in the one case the blowing of a butterfly's "dye-dusty" wing against the poet's cheek, in the other the shaking down of snow "dust" upon the poet by a crow. These are moments of unstated grace, in which the poet is saved, if only momentarily, from himself—saved, one might venture, from the "considerations" to which he would refer in "Birches."

It is not entirely far-fetched to invoke Job at this point, especially given Frost's long-standing interest in that particular book of the Old Testament, as evidenced by the long dramatic poem *A Masque of Reason* (1945). "My soul is weary of my life; I will leave my complaint upon myself; I will speak in the bitterness of my soul" (10:1). "Remember, I beseech thee, that thou hast made me as the clay; and wilt thou bring me into dust again?" (10:9).

> I am afraid of all my sorrows, I know that thou wilt not hold me innocent.
> If I be wicked, why then labour I in vain?
> If I wash myself with snow water, and make my hands never so clean;
> Yet shalt thou plunge me in the ditch, and mine own clothes shall abhor me. [9:28–31]

If Job is pertinent to Frost's two poems, then it is so not only in the reference to snow but also in the reminder of man's mortality—that he will be returned to dust. This heavy note of mortality is obviously present in "My Butterfly," with its "gray grass . . . , scarce dappled with the snow," and its final lines:

> I found that wing withered to-day;
> For you are dead, I said,
> And the strange birds say.
> I found it with the withered leaves
> Under the eaves.

Something of the same note of mortality inheres a bit insidiously in the image of "dust of snow."

In both poems, however, there is an attempt to communicate a sense of grace. "Some part of a day" the poet "had rued" has been saved because the poet's "heart" has been given "a change of mood." The "wild touch" of the butterfly's "dye-dusty wing" is somehow ameliorating before the "conspiracy" that was "rife" against the poet's "life."

It is characteristic of Frost that he should discover such moments of grace in the entirely ordinary moments of quotidian life. In this respect, it may be instructive to compare his moments with a similar moment in the experience of Carl Jung. For both of them the visitation comes from the skies.

> I thought it over again and arrived at the same conclusion. "Obviously God also desires me to show courage," I thought. "If that is so and I go through with it, then He will give me His grace and illumination."

I gathered all my courage, as though I were about to leap forthwith into hell-fire, and let the thought come. I saw before me the cathedral, the blue sky. God sits on His golden throne, high above the world—and from under the throne an enormous turd falls upon the sparkling new roof, shatters it, and breaks the walls of the cathedral asunder.

So that was it! I felt an enormous, an indescribable relief. Instead of the expected damnation, grace had come upon me, and with it an unutterable bliss such as I had never known. I wept for happiness and gratitude. The wisdom and goodness of God had been revealed to me now that I had yielded to his inexorable command. It was as though I had experienced an illumination.[5]

Nothing "enormous" is required, just "dust of snow."

Yet there is also a more strident Frost, one who would challenge the elements to get in his way, to stop him in his both literal and figural tracks. In "Dust in the Eyes," however, we no longer encounter anything resembling grace. Published in *West-Running Brook* (1928), this poem reads:

> If, as they say, some dust thrown in my eyes
> Will keep my talk from getting overwise,
> I'm not the one for putting off the proof.
> Let it be overwhelming, off a roof
> And round a corner, blizzard snow for dust,
> And blind me to a standstill if it must.[6]

Hence the paradox that out of dust comes clarification, as, in a sense, it does in "The Oven Bird."

Over time it has become increasingly evident that this sonnet struck a note which became central to the work of many of the major poets of the first quarter of the twentieth century. Anticipating the sorrowful observation of his younger contemporary T.S. Eliot, that in our time the ancient song of the nightingale had degenerated into the "Jug Jug" of dirty ears, Frost focused on the transformation and diminution of Whitman's central symbol for the poet. In the midsummer, midwood song of the ovenbird, Frost hears a parable of the modern poet who, unlike those poets who can burst into song only in the spring, has learned the ovenbird's paradoxical trick. He has learned how to sing an unlyrical song in those times that are not at all conducive to joyous song.

There is a singer everyone has heard,
Loud, a mid-summer and a mid-wood bird,
Who makes the solid tree trunks sound again.
He says that leaves are old and that for flowers
Mid-summer is to spring as one to ten.
He says the early petal-fall is past
When pear and cherry bloom went down in showers
On sunny days a moment overcast;
And comes that other fall we name the fall.
He says the highway dust is over all.
The bird would cease and be as other birds
But that he knows in singing not to sing.
The question that he frames in all but words
Is what to make of a diminished thing.

When "The Oven Bird" was published in *Mountain Interval* (1916), Frost's third collection of poems, its reception among readers displeased the poet. That reception drove him to warn his friend Sidney Cox that "The Oven Bird" was not of "the large things in the book." He cautioned further, obviously worried over the unsubtle impact of the poem's last two lines, "You mustn't be misled by anything that may have been laid down to you in school into exaggerating the importance of a little sententious tag to a not over important poem."[7] What other readers found in the poem is evident from Frost's complaint to Elizabeth Shepley Sergeant that the last two lines of his poem had "been used unjustly against New England."[8] Just *how* they had been misused Frost apparently chose not to explain to Mrs. Sergeant, nor did he wish to explain that his poem was purely in the New England tradition. There is no denying the validity of Mrs. Sergeant's emphasis upon "the tragic background of the poet who writes from the heart of the life that he knows and divines";[9] but much of the varied, rich life the poet knew, divined, and portrayed, it should be observed, shows the impact of the books he read and chose to love. Fully alert to classical Western literary traditions, Frost was acutely aware of the romantic tradition of New England, whose poets, in the flowering of New England literature, opened the way for Frost's own poetry of embattlement and resistance in addition to blazing a path followed by dozens of lesser writers.

The New England context of Frost's poem has never been fully investigated. In the paragraphs which follow, I shall try to locate some of the immediate sources for Frost's decision to turn the ovenbird into a surrogate for the poet. Clear hints for the ovenbird as symbol, I shall maintain, came from three writers (though there may have been others) whose work varies greatly in intrinsic literary merit—Henry David Thoreau, Bradford Torrey (Thoreau's editor at the turn of the century), and Mildred Howells (the daughter of William Dean Howells). The line can be drawn chronologically.

Reimagining his dramatic withdrawal to the Concord woods, Thoreau laments the fate that, in the few years since his removal, has befallen the woods encircling Walden Pond: "the woodchoppers have still further laid them waste, and now for many a year there will be no more rambling through the aisles of the wood, with occasional vistas through which you see the water. My Muse may be excused if she is silent henceforth." As nature's poet, then, Thoreau would fall as silent as the disappointed songbirds, for diminished nature—in this case, nature reduced through man's waste—silences both Muse and mortal song. "How can you expect the birds to sing," entones Thoreau, "when their groves are cut down?"[10]

In *Walden* Thoreau fails to identify the ovenbird by name, but his journals contain several descriptions of the ovenbird and its sounds, along with several related descriptions of a "night-warbler." At various times Thoreau observes, in notes that were not lost on Frost, that (1) "the oven-bird thrums [a] sawyer-like strain," (2) "the hollow-sounding note of the ovenbird is heard from the depth of the wood," (3) the oven-bird's note is "loud and unmistakable, making the hollow woods ring," (4) its note, a true "woodland" sound, is "fresh emphatic."[11] Thoreau suggests that he was able to distinguish the seasonal songs of the ovenbird, though he makes nothing of that fact.

Thoreau was as receptive to the ovenbird's spring song, evidently, as he was to its midsummer song. But his puzzlement sometimes led him to ascribe the two songs to different species. Often mistaking the ovenbird for a different bird he chose to call a "night-warbler," he wrote enthusiastically about that "powerful singer": "It launches into the air above the forest, or over some hollow or open space in the woods, and challenges the attention of the woods by its rapid and impetuous warble, and then drops down swiftly into the tree-tops like a performer withdrawing behind the scenes, and he is very lucky who detects where it alights."[12] For all his repute as a naturalist, Thoreau never managed to distinguish the ovenbird satisfactorily from the mysterious "night-warbler," confusing them time and time again. It is now generally conceded by ornithologists and Thoreau scholars alike that Thoreau's "mysterious" night-warbler and the seemingly different ovenbird, whose more characteristic song and daytime appearance were well known to Thoreau, were one and the same.[13]

That the ovenbird sings two quite different songs was clear enough to Bradford Torrey. In 1900, while editing Thoreau's journals, Torrey wrote and published a Thoreauvian journey piece. Reconstructing the memorable incidents of a day's excursion to New Hampshire's Franconia Mountains (where Frost would later live), Torrey wrote of the ovenbird:

An oven-bird shoots into the air out of the forest below for a burst of aerial afternoon music. I heard the preluding strain, and, glancing up, caught him at once, the sunlight happening to strike him perfectly. All the morning he has been speaking prose; now he is a poet; a division of the day from which the rest of us might take a lesson. But for his afternoon role he needs a name. "Oven-bird" goes somewhat heavily in a lyric:

"Hark! hark! the *oven-bird* at heaven's gate sings"—you would hardly recognize that for Shakespeare.[14]

Torrey notes with accuracy that the ovenbird can and does sing two distinctly different songs. The distinction between the songs is explained by one of Thoreau's modern editors. The ovenbird's "song is a series of short, ringing, emphatic notes that grow louder and louder as the tempo increases," she observes. "It is often called the teacher-bird because the song sounds like *teacher* repeated over and over again. The Ovenbird also has a beautiful flight song, most often heard in May and June, late in the afternoon or on moonlight nights."[15]

For his own purposes Frost chose the ovenbird whose song is pedagogical, not lyrical. He reverses Torrey's emphasis, which was on the lyrical beauty of the afternoon song. Surely Torrey's view of the ovenbird was too conventional for Frost's more insistent taste and therefore wholly unsuited to the specific purposes of his parablelike poem. In Frost there is, of course, no indication that the ovenbird sings a beautiful flight song as well as the dry, sharp, rasping song for which it is better known. The existence of its melodious flight song is a fact not at all useful to the poet answering the sentimentalist whose song falters and fails before natural loss.

On one occasion Frost revealed that his poems were largely "a way *out* of something." He elaborated: "I could probably name twenty or thirty poems that were just answers to somebody that had . . . left me unsatisfied with the last thing he said in an argument."[16] The possibility can be entertained, for its suggestive implications at least, that "The Oven Bird" constitutes just such an answer to the question framed by Mildred Howells in her Keatsian poem, " 'And No Birds Sing' ":

> There comes a season when the bird is still
> >Save for a broken note, so sad and strange,
> Its plaintive cadence makes the woodlands thrill
> >With sense of coming change.
>
> Stirred into ecstasy by spring's new birth,
> >In throbbing rhapsodies of hope and love,
> He shared his transports with the listening earth
> >And stormed the heavens above.
>
> But now how should he sing—forlorn, alone—
> >Of hopes that withered with the waning year,
> An empty nest with mate and fledgelings flown,
> >And winter drawing near?[17]

There can be no doubt, of course, that in quality, no matter what yardstick we use, Miss Howells's autumn poem does not measure up to Frost's. For one thing, it lacks immediate force and overall resonance. Its images too evidently belong to the pale, late Victorian poetry of nature. They remain static and generalized. Still, despite reservations, there is value and purpose in comparing the two poems. Sentimentality and loose structure notwithstanding, Miss Howells's poem does indicate a theme that Frost would find congenial: how, indeed, does one respond to the diminished thing that dry midsummer augurs and which autumn and winter all too surely realize?

The first line of Frost's sonnet seems to echo and answer the first line of " 'And No Birds Sing' ": "There is a singer everyone has heard" counters the line, "There comes a season when the bird is still." Moreover, if a "broken note . . . of plaintive cadence" predicts "coming change" in the Howells poem, the sterner song of Frost's ovenbird, in describing facts as they are, "makes the solid tree trunks sound again."

The middle stanza of Miss Howells's poem moves back in time to recall the retrospective irony of the bird's ecstasy when it was fostered by "spring's new birth." By contrast, in midpoem Frost's ovenbird reminds us dryly and matter-of-factly that spring's luxuriance of flowers diminishes by midsummer in the ratio of "one to ten." Then in the eleventh line Frost fashions another answer to " 'And No Birds Sing.' " The question asked in the Howells poem, "how should he sing" of withered hopes in a "waning year" as winter encroaches upon life, is answered: the ovenbird "knows in singing not to sing." Frost concludes his poem, not by asking Howells's question of whether the ovenbird *should* sing (he takes it for granted that he *must* sing) but by defining the question which the bird's songless song frames.

Like his ovenbird of midsummer song, the poet that Frost continued to recognize in himself was one who faced the hardest of facts: seasonally, but above all historically, the world has diminished, and "dust is over all." Still, the difficulty of the situation cannot reduce the durable poet to compliance: he resists the fact, and his resistance becomes the impulse—bone and sinew—for his poem. When Frost decided that "a poet must lean hard on facts, so hard, sometimes, that they hurt,"[18] he discovered as well that what "the facts do to you . . . transforms them into poetry."[19]

In seasons of human displacement, the Muse will continue to spite Thoreau (and his less durable followers) by disdaining silence. Transposed to a different key, it will speak but only to that poet whose lyric voice has been stripped of all traditional lyricism.

ELEVEN

Swinging

> When I am at the top I always find myself alone. Nobody speaks to me; the frost of loneliness makes me shiver. What do I want up high?
> —Friedrich Nietzsche, *Also Sprach Zarathustra* (1883)

SEVERAL TIMES in *Robert Frost: A Living Voice,* his account of the poet's talks at the Bread Loaf School of English, Reginald L. Cook quotes Frost's remarks on "Birches." Frost's words on one such occasion are given a context by Cook, who writes:

In spite of his deprecatory view of explication, Frost revealed a good deal about his art. When he disclosed his feeling about certain words in "Birches," he gave a searching insight into what makes a poet's use of descriptive words stand up. And how cavalierly he did it! He offered "this little note on 'Birches' before I begin to read it. See. The kind of explication I forbid," he said self-consciously. Then with disarming slyness, he said: "I never go down the shoreline [from Boston] to New York without watching the birches to see if they live up to what I say about them in the poem." Invariably the listener laughed, but on the double take he realized that Frost, the careful craftsman, was confirming his assertion that birches bend to left and right *by verification.* Getting details right was a telling responsibility. His birches, he insisted, were *not* the white mountain or paper birch of northern New England (*Betula papyrifera*); they were the gray birch (*Betula populifolia*).[1]

Frost does not say so, but his remarks could have been appropriately directed to those editors and designers of *The Pocket Book of Robert Frost's Poems* (Cardinal edition), published in 1953. The illustration on the cover is of ten "white" birches, eight of them leaning uniformly to the right and the other two, one at either end, standing straight. Given the popularity of this thirty-five-cent paperback, it is no wonder that the poet would want to set the record straight.

From the time of its first publication in the *Atlantic Monthly* in August 1915 and its reprinting in William Stanley Braith-waite's *Anthology of Magazine Verse for 1915*, "Birches" has been one of Frost's best known and most widely valued poems. It has also been close to the top of any list of the poet's most studied poems, with criticism divided as to the poem's merits and alleged deficiencies. If the most persistent question centers on whether the poet has earned the uplifting sentiments that emerge from his ruminations and speculation about birches, boys, and ice storms, it is nevertheless the case that the poem continues to call for interpretation and explanation and that this remains so despite Randall Jarrell's comment that the poem always leaves us a taste that is "a little brassy, a little sugary."[2]

The way in which Robert Frost came to write "Birches" is described by Elizabeth Shepley Sergeant: "As for the poet, 'who never saw New England as clearly as when he was in Old England,' he could not tie down his creative moments. It was about this time, early in 1914, while tramping the muddy yard at the Bungalow [West Midlands], that he suddenly, he says, wrote a new poem, not to be included in *North of Boston*. This was the now so famous and beloved 'Birches,' with its cold and crystal memories of another kind of wintry world."[3] As this account suggests, Frost's poem might have reflected pure, almost spontaneous invention, but if so, it was stimulated by memories of boyhood experiences of winter and summer in northern New England and sharpened by the perspective of the poet's self-imposed exile. What I would suggest, however, is that in "Birches," even though Frost saw New England most clearly when he was in Old England, he re-viewed his wintry New England scene through Thoreauvian eyes.

On December 31, 1852, a day of rain and ice in Concord, Thoreau wrote in his *Journals* with keen anticipation: "It is a sort of frozen rain this afternoon, which does not wet one, but makes the still bare ground slippery with a coating of ice, and stiffens your umbrella so that it cannot be shut. Will not the trees look finely in the morning?"[4] For the next few days Thoreau described the storm's "fine" effects upon the landscape. On the first day of the new year he observed: "This morning we have something between ice and frost on the trees. . . . What a crash of jewels as you walk! . . . The drooping birches along the edges of woods are the most feathery, fairy-like ostrich plumes of the trees, and the color of their trunks increases the delusion" (436-38). The next day Thoreau continued his report:

In this clear air and bright sunlight, the ice-covered trees have a new beauty, especially the birches . . . , bent quite to the ground in every kind of curve. At a distance, as you are approaching them endwise, they look like white tents of Indians under the edge of the wood. The birch is thus remarkable, perhaps, because from the feathery form of the tree, whose numerous small branches sustain so great a weight, bending it to the ground, and moreover because, from the color of the bark, the core is less observable. The oaks not only are less pliant in the trunk, but have fewer and stiffer twigs and branches. The birches droop over in all directions, like ostrich-feathers. [440]

Thoreau's description anticipates Frost's handling of imagery. But Thoreau's entry the next day offers an interesting variation on Frost's poem. He begins by recording that day's response to the observable beauty which can be attributed to nature's transforming and creative powers and then speculates on the comparative merits of man and nature. The first paragraph is largely descriptive of this "finest show of ice" (444): "Nothing dark met the eye, but a silvery sheen, precisely as if the whole tree—trunk, boughs, and twigs—were converted into burnished silver. You exclaimed at every hedgerow. Sometimes a clump of birches fell over every way in graceful ostrich-plumes, all raying from one centre. . . . Suddenly all is converted to crystal. The world is a crystal palace" (445).

The next paragraph, however, moves into a new key. Stimulated by his last attempt at describing ice-laden birches, Thoreau ruminates:

I love Nature partly *because* she is not man, but a retreat from him. None of his institutions control or pervade her. There a different kind of right prevails. In her midst I can be glad with an entire gladness. If this world were all man, I could not stretch myself, I should lose all hope. He is constraint, she is freedom to me. He makes me wish for another world. She makes me content with this. . . .

> Man, man is the devil,
> The source of evil . . . .

I have a room all to myself; it is nature. It is a place beyond the jurisdiction of human governments. . . . There are two worlds, the post-office and nature. I know them both. I continually forget mankind and their institutions, as I do a bank. [445-46]

The conjunction of Thoreau's celebration of winter birches and his buoyant homily on man's inferiority to nature may be compared with Frost's similar conjunction of themes in "Birches." If man makes Thoreau "wish for another world" but nature makes him "content with this," to Frost it is when life most resembles nature—when "life is too much like a pathless wood"—that the poet would "like to get away from earth awhile." Frost would "climb black branches up a snow-white trunk / *Toward* heaven," but he would come back, he quickly decides, for "Earth's the right place for love." Thoreau would undoubtedly endorse Frost's aphorism. But their initial agreement would evaporate, I suspect, if each were to explain precisely what he took the statement to mean. While Thoreau would most characteristically focus on love of nature, Frost would just as readily assert the claim of man's fundamental love for man. The distinction is notable.

In the *Journal* passages that I have quoted above, Thoreau (for the moment read "man") appears almost exclusively as an observer, never as a participant beyond the act of perception. It is as if in nature's pure realm man's existence were suspended. Whenever Thoreau does tell in these entries what men are doing, or what they have done, he invariably does so to admonish them. Consequently, when he "climb[s] the bank at Stow's wood-lot and come[s] upon the piles of freshly split white pine wood," he does not compliment the worker for his labor, as one might expect, but decides, rather, that the owner of the woodlot is "ruthlessly laying it waste" (441). And in the same entry, a page or so later, he comments on the ringing of bells: "The bells are particularly sweet this morning. I hear more, methinks, than ever before. How much more religion in their sound, than they ever call men together to! Men obey their call and go to the stove-warmed church, though God exhibits himself to the walker in a frosted bush to-day, as much as in a burning one to Moses of old" (443). Even when man does something well (after all, bells are a human invention), he is singularly capable of misinterpreting his own message and betraying his most noble purposes. For Thoreau the beauty and divinity which exist at this moment are in the glazed birch and the frosted bush. They are most certainly not in men. Nature and nature's workings are at the center of creation. In these pages Thoreau reserves his approval for the landscape transformed by ice and snow, and the few men who make an appearance intrude momentarily along nature's periphery.

In Frost's poem, however, values are weighted somewhat differently. Its first twenty lines are largely devoted to a description of the effect ice-storms have on birches:

> When I see birches bend to left and right
> Across the lines of straighter darker trees,
> I like to think some boy's been swinging them.
> But swinging doesn't bend them down to stay
> As ice-storms do. Often you must have seen them
> Loaded with ice a sunny winter morning
> After a rain. They click upon themselves
> As the breeze rises, and turn many-colored
> As the stir cracks and crazes their enamel.
> Soon the sun's warmth makes them shed crystal shells
> Shattering and avalanching on the snow-crust—
> Such heaps of broken glass to sweep away
> You'd think the inner dome of heaven had fallen.
> They are dragged to the withered bracken by the load,
> And they seem not to break; though once they are bowed
> So low for long, they never right themselves:
> You may see their trunks arching in the woods
> Years afterwards, trailing their leaves on the ground
> Like girls on hands and knees that throw their hair
> Before them over their heads to dry in the sun.[5]

The details in these lines are precise and deceptively neutral. The entire passage contains nothing to suggest that nature is superior (or inferior) to man, nor are we to infer that the two are equal. As description these lines exemplify what Frost calls the "matter-of-fact" of "Truth." But Frost does not stop with the conclusion that ice storms, and not swinging boys, are the cause of birches bent "down to stay." He approaches, finally, the idea that man's acts upon nature have their own meaning and beauty: approvingly Frost decides that, given a choice, he "should prefer to have some boy bend" birches. In the midst of swinging, boys are not observers of nature; they actually collaborate with nature by taking the "stiffness" out of birches. Frost would have a bent tree signify that some boy, swinging from earth, has gone beyond that "pathless wood / Where your face burns and tickles with the cobwebs / Broken across it." "Birches" suggests that nature's beauty is somehow enhanced when man has worked an effect upon nature. In this sense Frost's poem may stand as a qualified reply to Thoreau's recurrent strain of illimitable nature worship.

Of course there is another side to Thoreau with which "Birches" does not conflict. A Thoreau more congenial to Frost appears in a *Journal* entry six months before the notable ice storm of December 31, 1852. He writes: "Nature must be viewed humanly to be viewed at all; that is, her scenes must be associated with humane affections, such as are associated with one's native place, for instance. She is most significant to a lover. A lover of Nature is preeminently a lover of man. If I have no friend, what is Nature to me? She ceases to be morally significant" (163). For Thoreau this kind of bravely humanistic sentiment welled forth most clearly on an early summer's day. The dead of winter, we have seen, could evoke other feelings. But Frost's humanism became a harder, more durable thing in its midwinter setting of ice and snow.

As late as August 1919, in a list of poems that his friend John T. Bartlett might like to read, Frost recommended "Swinging Birches."[6] In some ways it is unfortunate that Frost stopped calling the poem by this title. I say unfortunate because the activity at the heart of the poem—the activity that generates whatever cohesion the poem has—is the boy's swinging of birches and the poet's ruminations on the possibility that the birches he sees have been bent by boys at play. He would like to think that such is the case. But since liking to think does not make it so, the poet turns to the more likely reason, the permanent bending of birches by ice storms.

> You may see their trunks arching in the woods
> Years afterwards, trailing their leaves on the ground
> Like girls on hands and knees that throw their hair
> Before them over their heads to dry in the sun.

Then, interrupting this train of thought—this "matter-of-fact" "Truth"—he returns to a consideration of the notion that by "swinging" them boys also bend trees (though not permanently, as ice storms do).

> I should prefer to have some boy bend them
> As he went out and in to fetch the cows—
> Some boy too far from town to learn baseball,
> Whose only play was what he found himself,
> Summer or winter, and could play alone.

Here the poem shifts into a generalized description, a semi-dramatic account of the way such a boy proceeds:

> One by one he subdued his father's trees
> By riding them down over and over again
> Until he took the stiffness out of them,
> And not one but hung limp, not one was left
> For him to conquer. He learned all there was
> To learn about not launching out too soon
> And so not carrying the tree away
> Clear to the ground. He always kept his poise
> To the top branches, climbing carefully
> With the same pains you use to fill a cup
> Up to the brim, and even above the brim.
> Then he flung outward, feet first, with a swish,
> Kicking his way down through the air to the ground.

At this point the poet acknowledges that he, too, was once "a swinger of birches," and he admits that even now he dreams of being one again. When does he have such dreams?

> It's when I'm weary of considerations,
> And life is too much like a pathless wood
> Where your face burns and tickles with the cobwebs
> Broken across it, and one eye is weeping
> From a twig's having lashed across it open.

To what sort of boyhood pleasure would the adult poet like to return? Quite simply, it is the pleasure of onanism. We do not need either Erica Jong or John Updike to remind us that "flying" is often a dream or linguistic substitute for sexual activity.[7] But we do need to be reminded that "early orgasms at puberty induced by friction against a tree trunk" are "not an uncommon experience," to quote from a writer commenting on the following passage from the early diaries of James Boswell: "Already (age 12-13) in climbing trees, pleasure. Could not conceive what it was. Thought of heaven. Returned often, climbed, felt, allowed myself to fall from high branches in ecstasy—all natural. Spoke of it to the gardener. He, rigid, did not explain."[8]

If physiologically there is some sort of pubescent sexuality taking place in the "swinging" of "birches," it is not surprising, then, that the boy has "subdued his father's trees" by "riding them down over and over again" until "not one was left for him to conquer" and that the orgasmic activity should be likened to "riding," which despite the "conquering" can be done time and again. One need only note that the notion of "riding," already figurative in "Birches," reappears metaphorically in Frost's conception of "Education by Poetry," wherein he writes: "Unless you are at home in the metaphor, unless you have had your proper poetical education in the metaphor, you are not safe anywhere. Because you are not at ease with figurative values: you don't know . . . how far you may expect to ride it and when it may break down with you."[9] And what is true for metaphor and poetry is true for love. Frost insisted that a poem "run . . . from delight to wisdom. The figure is the same as for love. Like a piece of ice on a hot stove the poem must ride on its own melting."[10] Then it is totally appropriate within the metaphor of "swinging birches" that even the storm-bent trees should look to the adult male like "girls on hands and knees that throw their hair / Before them over their heads to dry in the sun." No wonder, then, and fully appropriate it is, that when the poet thinks that his wish to get away from earth might by some fate be misunderstood such that he be snatched away never to return, his thought is that "Earth's the right place for love." At some level of his consciousness the pleasurable activity of "swinging birches" has transformed itself into the more encompassing term "love." One might say, within the logic of this reading of the poem, that "Earth's the right place for [sexual] love," including onanistic love. The same sexual metaphor runs through the final lines of the poem as the mature poet thinks of how he would like to go but only to come back.

> I'd like to go by climbing a birch tree,
> And climb black branches up a snow-white trunk
> *Toward* heaven, till the tree could bear no more,
> But dipped its top and set me down again.
> That would be good both going and coming back.
> One would do worse than be a swinger of birches.

In "swinging" birches the boy brings form (although only temporarily) to the trees. He does it by himself, too far from other boys for a pickup game of baseball. It is a lesser kind of form that the boy throws off, but undoubtedly pleasing and engrossing, both in the going and in the coming. "Fortunately, too, no forms are more engrossing, gratifying, comforting, staying, than those lesser ones we throw off," wrote Frost in a letter to the *Amherst Student* in 1935; "like vortex rings of smoke, all our individual enterprise and needing nobody's cooperation: a basket, a letter, a garden, a room, an idea, a picture, a poem. For these we haven't to get a team together before we can play."[11] To these forms, on the basis of what goes on in "Birches," we can add onanism. The doubleness of the pleasure for the boy—new form for the supple trees and sexual pleasure for himself—

shows this poem to be linked in an unexpected way to "Two Tramps in Mud Time," where the poet decides:

> My object in living is to unite
> My avocation and my vocation
> As my two eyes make one in sight.
> Only where love and need are one,
> And the work is play for mortal stakes,
> Is the deed ever really done
> For Heaven and the future's sakes.[12]

Here too are "love" and "play" done for "Heaven['s]" sake, even as the boy bender of birches "climb[s] black branches up a snow-white trunk / *Toward* heaven, till the tree could bear no more, / But dipped its top and set me down again." Tumescence and detumescence? Or merely *like* tumescence and detumescence? Metaphor or the act itself? By this time in the poem it does not much matter, for "that would be good both going and coming back." Thoreau's metaphor for such double gratification, engrossment, was in the chopping of wood. It warmed him twice, both in the chopping and in the burning.

Anyone who ever attended one of Frost's performances can readily visualize the "rare twinkle of his grave blue eyes" (Wilfred Gibson's expression)[13] as he finished reading this poem to his most appreciative audience. To the summer audiences at Bread Loaf when he recited "Birches" he took to talking about what impressed him about the poem. On one occasion he called attention to the word "crazes" in the line "As the stir cracks and crazes their enamel."[14] But the word he kept coming back to was in another line. It would take "a masterpiece of explication to say," he insisted, "the line that probably means most to me now is 'It's when I'm weary of considerations.' "[15] The word in that sentence upon which he would fasten was "considerations." On another occasion he added that the line meant most to him *now.* "That's when you get older. It didn't mean so much to me when I wrote it as it does now."[16] To still another audience, he addressed the rhetorical question: "You see, did you notice the emphasis laid on 'weary considerations'? See. It just means you're getting weary of all things that pair off—lone-

liness, togetherness, lone-wolfness. I'm sick of having to consid-
er the lone-wolfness and the togetherness. Those horrible
words! Somebody manufactured one, and I manufactured the
other."[17] It is typical of Frost to call attention to an otherwise
unnoticed word in a familiar poem, insist on its great value to
himself, and then deflect understanding of the word in some
seemingly idiosyncratic way.

Frost was sick at times, he would tell us, of being "consider-
ate" of others. Yet it is entirely possible that "considerations"—
as used in "Birches"—resonates in other famous Frost poems,
such as "Desert Places," "A Star in a Stone-Boat," "All Revela-
tion," and "Stars." Frost once defined poetry as "the renewal of
words."[18] Latinist that he was, Frost could not have been un-
aware that "consider" derives from *considerare*, to observe (orig-
inally a term of augury meaning "to observe the stars care-
fully"). In "Bond and Free," the poem which immediately pre-
cedes "Birches" in *Mountain Interval*, Frost concludes in the
second half of the poem:

> Thought cleaves the interstellar gloom
> And sits in Sirius' disc all night,
> Till day makes him retrace his flight,
> With smell of burning on every plume,
> Back past the sun to an earthly room.
>
> His gains in heaven are what they are.
> Yet some say Love by being thrall
> And simply staying possesses all
> In several beauty that Thought fares far
> To find fused in another star.[19]

Against the counterclaims of "Thought" and "Love"—stars and
earth—we can look at a different Frost poem.

It was to the subject of loneliness that he turned later in one
of his most famous poems, "Desert Places." Emerson had writ-
ten in *Nature*: "The greatest delight which the fields and woods
minister, is the suggestion of an occult relation between man
and the vegetable. I am not alone and unacknowledged. They
nod to me and I to them. The waving of the boughs in the storm,

is new to me and old."[20] He had also written in *Nature*: "What new thoughts are suggested by seeing a face of country quite familiar, in the rapid movements of the rail-road car!"[21] In "Desert Places" Frost follows the hint in the latter statement in order to make a discovery about himself that he can throw up against Emerson's buoyant assertion that there exists an "occult relation between man and the vegetable."

> Snow falling and night falling fast, oh, fast
> In a field I looked into going past,
> And the ground almost covered smooth in snow,
> But a few weeds and stubble showing last.
>
> The woods around it have it—it is theirs.
> All animals are smothered in their lairs.
> I am too absent-spirited to count;
> The loneliness includes me unawares.
>
> And lonely as it is that loneliness
> Will be more lonely ere it will be less—
> A blanker whiteness of benighted snow
> With no expression, nothing to express.
>
> They cannot scare me with their empty spaces
> Between stars—on stars where no human race is.
> I have it in me so much nearer home
> To scare myself with my own desert places.[22]

Earth is the right place for love. Given the desert stars and the empty spaces between them, it might well be the only place. As Frost concluded elsewhere, "There is apparently not a soul but us alive in the whole business of rolling balls[,] eddying fires, and long distance rays of light. It makes any cozyness in our nook here all the more heart-warming."[23]

Frost tried to coach his readers regarding the possible initial circumstances that led up to the poem we now know as "Birches." It began in an observation possibly, quite like an observation made from a moving vehicle, perhaps a train, of permanently bent birch trees. Of course, the poem begins this way, generalizing, as it goes: "When I see birches bend to left and right." To audiences he would later present the natural observations, it will be recalled, that the birches along the shoreline to New York did "live up" to what he said about them in the poem.[24] He does not quite make the full claim, but what was he looking to confirm by so much observation, if not that nature imitated art, that nature's birches did bend "to left and right" as they did in the poet's poem?

PART THREE

Mainly Emerson

TWELVE

Nature's Gold

[The poet's] true nectar . . . is the ravishment of the
intellect by coming nearer to the fact.
—Ralph Waldo Emerson, "The Poet" (1844)

IN *Nature*, at the beginning of the section on "Language," Emerson writes down his audacious syllogism:
1. Words are signs of natural facts.
2. Particular natural facts are symbols of particular spiritual facts.
3. Nature is the symbol of spirit.[1]

Later on, Emerson insists: "A Fact is the end or last issue of spirit."[2] Frost put it another way: "The fact is the sweetest dream that labor knows."[3]

There is almost too much in *Nature* about what particularly and spiritually matters to be helpful in our understanding of the specifics of a poem such as Frost's "Mowing." Either directly or somewhat obliquely, much of what Emerson says in this great essay can be made to apply to the poem. But we can limit ourselves to a few sentences, this time from "Prospects," the final section, wherein Emerson writes:

The invariable mark of wisdom is to see the miraculous in the common. What is a day? What is a year? What is summer? What is woman? What is a child? What is sleep? To our blindness, these things seem unaffecting. We make fables to hide the baldness of the fact and conform it, as we say, to the higher law of the mind. But when the fact is seen under the light of an idea, the gaudy fable fades and shrivels. We behold the real higher law. To the wise, therefore, a fact is true poetry, and the most beautiful of fables.[4]

Whatever else "Mowing" is about, it deals with "the miraculous in the common"—the commonness of "mowing," of poetic meditation upon the nature and value of one's own labor. Once the mowing is done, the hay will make itself, and that should be reward enough for a farmer—but not so for the farmer who is also a poet. Like the Thoreau who would not only know beans but would also cultivate metaphors even as he worked the earth, Frost must derive more from mowing than just hay. He will search, if not for objects, then for meaning, and he fastens upon the long scythe's "whispering"—a whispering that, significantly, is directed not at the poet but "to the ground." What does the scythe whisper? asks the poet.

> Perhaps it was something about the heat of the sun,
> Something, perhaps, about the lack of sound—
> And that was why it whispered and did not speak.
> It was no dream of the gift of idle hours,
> Or easy gold at the hand of fay or elf[.]

But these are fables the poet makes up about the fact of the sound made by the scythe in his hands—"fables to hide the baldness of the fact and conform it, as we say, to the higher law of the mind." Yet they would constitute "more than the truth," as Frost has it, and "would have seemed too weak / To the earnest love that laid the swale in rows, / . . . and scared a bright green snake." Now, here Frost expresses an idea, and when the sounds made by the scythe (the immediate result and therefore emblematic of the poet's act of labor)—or rather fables the poet has constructed about the sound of that scythe—are "seen under the light of [that] idea," we see that "the gaudy fable fades and shrivels." The fact itself, the poet discovers, is "the sweetest dream that labor knows." That is not what the working scythe is whispering, for even the poet does not know that it "says" anything, at least not in so many words. But whether or not the sound of the scythe's whispering to the ground is "the noise of facts" (William James's phrase),[5] that sound has been the necessary cause for the poet's discovery of the aphorism with which, we may be surprised to recall, he chooses not to end his poem. In the movement of his scythe, as in the rhythm of his labor (and in the poem's as well), the farmer-poet illustrates Emerson's meaning when he wrote: "God offers to every mind its choice between truth and repose. Take which you please,—you can never have both. Between these, as a pendulum, man oscillates."[6] We do not know for certain in the end whether Frost's "fact" is "true poetry, and the most beautiful of fables," for Frost chooses to call it "the sweetest dream that labor knows." Is it only "dream" and therefore illusory, or is it "dream" in the ideal sense and therefore the capstone and reward for the labor to which man, because of the fall from Eden, is doomed?

In "Away!"—a late poem on the theme of imminent death (his own)—Frost writes:

> I leave behind
> Good friends in town.
> Let them get well-wined
> And go lie down.

> Don't think I leave
> For the outer dark
> Like Adam and Eve
> Put out of the Park.

> Forget the myth.[7]

In the last year of his life, the poet found himself, not in the midst of a dark wood, but, as he himself recognized in the title of his final collection of poems, *In the Clearing* (1962). It *was* time to forget the myth.

Several of Frost's finest poems through the years reflected his fascination with the myth of Adam and Eve and his preoccupation with the human consequences of their fall: what he called, in "Kitty Hawk," "Our instinctive venture / Into what they call / The material / When we took that fall / From the apple tree."[8] In "The Oven Bird" the attraction that the myth holds for him translates into the poetic idea that nature in New England annually reproduces its analogue of the fall of man. In "After Apple-Picking" the matter is handled a bit differently. There the poet-farmer describes his concern regarding the "coming on" of sleep which will end his long day's labor. For he knows that troubled sleep and repetitive dreams, resulting directly from the daytime activity which has brought him to the harvest and the "wealth" he covets, are his meed. The remembered sensations of apple picking—the "bodily memories of the experience (what we farmers used to call kinesthetic images)"[9]—will prevail in his sleep and will disturb his rest. In memory, but seemingly even stronger than memory, there will nag the "scent" of apples, the "sight" through the skimmed morning ice, the "ache" and "pressure" on the instep arch, the "hearing" of the "rumbling" from the cellar bin. "If you gather apples in the sunshine . . . and shut your eyes," wrote Emerson, "you shall still see apples hanging in the bright light."[10] In sum, Frost knows not whether that sleep will be like the animal hibernation (the "long sleep") of the woodchuck or, as the poet puts it ironically, "just some human sleep."[11]

The country details of "After Apple-Picking" only partly mask the poet's concern with the mythic consequences of the Fall. If Eve's curse, after she tasted of the fruit from the forbidden tree, was that she would "bring forth children," Adam's curse, after joining Eve in the risk, was that he would live henceforth by the "sweat" of his "face"—that is, he would sustain his life by his own labor. The irony beyond this curse is Frost's subject. Adam's curse was to labor, but another way of putting it is that Adam and his descendants were doomed to live within, and at the mercy of, the senses. Significantly, Frost defines the curse still further: man will not cease to labor even in rest.

In the very desire to profit from his long hours of work, the poet has made himself vulnerable, in a wry sense, to the dictum that "the sleep of a labouring man is sweet, whether he eat little or much; but the abundance of the rich will not suffer him to sleep" (Ecclesiastes 5:12). The rub is that the poet is both laborer and "rich" man. He has the "great harvest" he desired; but he has labored long and faithfully in bringing about that harvest—certainly *too* long and possibly *too* faithfully to enable him to reap the reward of peaceful, untroubled rest that is promised to the diligent laborer.

The poem can be seen as an elaboration of Genesis: Adam's

curse was not merely that he was doomed to live by the "sweat" of his "face" but also that the curse to labor would follow him into his rest and his dreams. Such, inevitably, is the way after apple picking—and such is the paradox of Adam's curse, even as it extends to the poet-farmer of New England.

But Thoreau had viewed man's curse in another way. "It is not necessary," he wrote in *Walden*, "that a man should earn his living by the sweat of his brow, unless he sweats easier than I do."[12] Indeed, as he had written earlier in *Walden*, the problem was that "men labor under a mistake. . . . [for] the better part of the man is soon ploughed into the soil for compost. By a seeming fate, commonly called necessity, they are employed, as it says in an old book, laying up treasures which moth and rust will corrupt and thieves break through and steal."[13] Behind Frost's poem, however, is the recognition of all that Thoreau says about man's misguided labors and bootless cupidity and, of course, in the person of the apple picker a tacit disregard of these injunctions from an "old book" and the new book that is *Walden*. Indeed, Frost's apple picker, "overtired / Of the great harvest" he has himself desired, has made the Thoreauvian mistake of being "so occupied with the factitious cares and superfluously coarse labors of life that its finer fruits cannot be plucked by them. Their fingers, from excessive toil, are too clumsy and tremble too much for that. . . . the laboring man . . . has no time to be anything but a machine. . . . The finest qualities of our nature, like the bloom on fruits, can be preserved only by the most delicate handling."[14] Something like Thoreau's admonitions, then, lies behind the uneasiness of Frost's apple picker's sleep ("One can see what will trouble / This sleep of mine, whatever sleep it is").

Thoreau, to illustrate his own labor ethic, describes his harvesting practices:

In October I went a-graping to the river meadows, and loaded myself with clusters more precious for their beauty and fragrance than for food. . . . The barberry's brilliant fruit was likewise food for my eyes merely; but I collected a small store of wild apples for coddling, which the proprietor and travellers had overlooked. When chestnuts were ripe

I laid up half a bushel for winter. It was very exciting at that season to roam the then boundless chestnut woods of Lincoln,—they now sleep their long sleep under the railroad,—with a bag on my shoulder, and a stick to open burrs with in my hand.[15]

The passage foreshadows Frost's "After Apple-Picking," of course, in the collection of the "small store of wild apples for coddling" and, rather remarkably, in the phrase, applied in Frost's poem to the woodchuck, the "long sleep." Another of Frost's "harvest" poems, "Unharvested," is also foreshadowed in the confession by Thoreau that his clusters of grapes were "more precious for their beauty and fragrance than for food."

> A scent of ripeness from over a wall.
> And come to leave the routine road
> And look for what had made me stall,
> There sure enough was an apple tree
> That had eased itself of its summer load,
> And of all but its trivial foliage free,
> Now breathed as light as a lady's fan.
> For there there had been an apple fall
> As complete as the apple had given man.
> The ground was one circle of solid red.
>
> May something go always unharvested!
> May much stay out of our stated plan,
> Apples or something forgotten and left,
> So smelling their sweetness would be no theft.[16]

In "After Apple-Picking" the poet-farmer had regretted those apples "That struck the earth," for "No matter if not bruised or spiked with stubble," they "Went surely to the cider-apple heap / As of no worth." In this different poem, "Unharvested," however, the poet realizes that such "falls" are of no concern to nature, nor should they be regretted by the poet. For in those "unharvested" apples there is the "harvest," as Thoreau had noted, of fragrance. The "summer load" of apples dropped unseen behind the wall gives off the "scent of ripeness"—the "sweetness"—that is the poet's harvest from the otherwise unharvested crop. These apples "have results," as Thoreau said of his beans, "which are not harvested by me."[17] There is an analogy here (in an odd way) to the abandoned woodpile of Frost's earlier poem. In deserting the woodpile he had so skillfully built, had not the woodman aped nature, which also creates and constructs in ways and for purposes that seemingly take no account of, and are perhaps even irrelevant for, man's creature needs and brutal purposes?

Exuberant at the advent of spring marked by the signs of melting snow and dissolving ice in the ponds, Thoreau welcomes the new (or at least renewed) creation:

The grass flames up on the hillsides like a spring fire . . ., as if the earth sent forth an inward heat to greet the returning sun; not yellow but green is the color of its flame;—the symbol of perpetual youth, the grass-blade, like a long green ribbon, streams from the sod into the summer, checked indeed by the frost, but anon pushing on again, lifting its spear of last year's hay with the fresh life below. It grows as steadily as the rill oozes out of the ground. It is almost identical with that, for in the growing days of June, when the rills are dry, the grass blades are their channels, and from year to year the herds drink at this perennial green stream, and the mower draws from it betimes their winter supply. So our human life but dies down to its root, and still puts forth its green blade to eternity.[18]

This green garden—this "new golden age" for all its brevity—attracts Frost as well but with a difference. His poem "Nothing Gold Can Stay" comments on a diminution already evident in the advent of nature's greenish green. By the time nature's flame is "not yellow but green," the fall from nature's grace has already taken place.

> Nature's first green is gold,
> Her hardest hue to hold.
> Her early leaf's a flower;
> But only so an hour.
> Then leaf subsides to leaf.
> So Eden sank to grief,
> So dawn goes down to day.
> Nothing gold can stay.[19]

Already in the passing from the green that is gold to the green that is green, we have well under way the process—fruition

followed by dessication—which by June will dry up the rills
(recall Frost's "Hyla Brook"—"By June our brook's run out of
song and speed"). Annually nature brings about the diminished
worth about which the oven-bird "knows in singing not to
sing." Thoreau sings gladly with the knowledge of spring about
summer and autumn and beyond. Frost sings dryly about the
dessication and death with which the gardens of spring are
already seeded. Yet once again, as the poet chooses to conclude
in "Hyla Brook," "We love the things we love for what they
are."[20]

THIRTEEN

Linked Analogies

Loved the wood-rose, and left it on its stalk.
—Ralph Waldo Emerson, "Forebearance" (1842)

CONCERNED ABOUT possible responses to his first collection of poems, *A Boy's Will* (1913), Frost set about hedging his bets. Fearing *under*interpretation above all, he provided straightforward hints to the themes of thirty of the thirty-two poems in the volume. After each entry in the table of contents he added a gloss. "The Demiurge's Laugh," for instance, carried the note that it is "about science," and "Pan with Us" is "about art (his own)." "The Tuft of Flowers" is "about fellowship."[1]

Encouraged by the reception accorded *A Boy's Will*, however, Frost found it unnecessary to add such glosses to his second collection, *North of Boston* (1914)—except in one case. "Mending Wall," opening the book, he prefaced with the statement that it "takes up the theme where 'A Tuft of Flowers' in *A Boy's Will* laid it down."[2] With this gesture Frost effectively linked the two books. Yet explicit though it is, the deliberately made connection between "The Tuft of Flowers" and "Mending Wall" has drawn little significant response from Frost's critics. The poems have *not* been read reflexively, that is, not fully in the light that each sheds upon the other, even though their author himself insisted upon the link.[3]

Frost would have the reader believe that, in writing "The Tuft of Flowers," he discovered the experience of renewed fellowship. "*A Boy's Will* told how I was scared away from life and crept back to it through this poem," Frost wrote; in "The Tuft of Flowers," he admitted, "I was speaking literally."[4] The experi-

ence had taught him, moreover, that fellowship transcends
time. It can exist between human beings who work the same
field but at different times. For in sparing the tuft of butterfly
weeds—"a leaping tongue of bloom"—the mower has per-
formed a deed that will communicate something of importance
to the worker who will follow him but not see him. At the
outset, the poet has decided: "I must be, as he had been,—
alone, / As all must be, I said within my heart, / 'Whether they
work together or apart.' "

There is considerable evidence that "The Tuft of Flowers" is
an Emersonian poem.[5] In the essay "Circles," Emerson democ-
ratizes the idea of the Christian Pentecost by identifying it with
inspired human conversation and friendship. That he would
compare ordinary conversation with the Holy Ghost's visit to
the disciples gives us some indication of the significance that
Emerson found in speech. But there is almost immediately a
rueful qualification. "The parties are not to be judged by the
spirit they partake and even express under this Pentecost,"
warns Emerson. "To-morrow they will have receded from this
high-water mark. To-morrow you shall find them stooping un-
der the old pack-saddles." And yet, he decides, "let us enjoy the
cloven flame whilst it glows on our walls."[6] The image of
"cloven flame" echoes Acts 2:3—"cloven tongues like as of
fire"; and as such, it offers a link between the New Testament
and Frost's poem, particularly in the image of the tuft of
flowers—"a leaping tongue of bloom." Frost's image is visual, of
course, but it is also allusive. In *speaking* to the poet, this
tongue, vaulting time, communicates just as Jesus' disciples did
when they "began to speak with other tongues, as the Spirit gave
them utterance" (2:4). In sparing the flowers, the now absent
mower has left his fellow worker a spiritual, Dionysian "mes-
sage from the dawn." Curiously enough, for Frost "brotherly
speech" has not involved "speech" at all. The mower's emblem-
atic gesture has conveyed Emersonian revelation symbolically.
"We all stand waiting, empty,—knowing, possibly, that we can
be full, surrounded by mighty symbols which are not symbols to
us, but prose and trivial toys," wrote Emerson. "Then cometh
the god, and converts the statues into fiery men, and by a flash of

his eye burns up the veil which shrouded all things, and the meaning of the very furniture, of cup and saucer, of chair and clock and tester, is manifest."[7]

There are other traces of "Circles" in Frost's poem. Beginning with conversation, Emerson moves on to a higher form of communication. "Good as is discourse, silence is better, and shames it," he decides. "The length of the discourse indicates the distance of thought betwixt the speaker and the hearer. If they were at a perfect understanding in any part, no words would be necessary thereon. If at one in all parts, no words would be suffered."[8] As Emerson had observed in *Nature*, "An action is the perfection and publication of thought. A right action seems to fill the eye, and to be related to all nature."[9] Frost's poem reaches further. It suggests something about the transcendental community shared by poets through their poetry. For poets and prophets, poems and prophecies are not merely words: they are gestures and actions. They, too, link workers who toil together even as they toil apart, and they bridge time as well as space. It is Whitman's gesture in "Crossing Brooklyn Ferry," though the image, as Frost uses it, comes from Emerson. Emerson's essays and poems are the "leaping tongue of bloom" that conveys "the message of the dawn" to the fellow poet who would follow and, in turn, lead. Literature, as Frost once defined it, consists of "words that have become deeds."[10]

"Mending Wall" is a meditative lyric that reports and assesses a dialogue between neighbors who have joined in the annual occupation of rebuilding the wall which separates their farms. Obviously antedating the farmers themselves, the old wall seems to serve no modern need. Has "walking the line" degenerated, the poet wonders, into bootless and vulgar ritual? Or are there fresh reasons, as yet unarticulated, for maintaining the wall? The poet's mischief—that impulse which urges him to needle his rather taciturn neighbor with this puckish question—acts to open things up.

Asked once about his intended meaning, Frost recast the question: "In my Mending Wall was my intention fulfilled with the characters portrayed and the atmosphere of the place?" Characteristically, he went on to answer obliquely.

I should be sorry if a single one of my poems stopped with either of those things—stopped anywhere in fact. My poems—I should suppose everybody's poems—are all set to trip the reader head foremost into the boundless. Ever since infancy I have had the habit of leaving my blocks carts chairs and such like ordinaries where people would be pretty sure to fall forward over them in the dark. Forward, you understand, *and* in the dark. I may leave my toys in the wrong place and so in vain. It is my intention we are speaking of—my innate mischievousness.[11]

No other poem in the Frost canon better illustrates his manner—as *he* described it—and his overall poetic intention. "Mending Wall" is constructed around the idea of mischief. The poet's mischief ultimately erects the verbal barrier that his neighbor is bullied into trying to surmount or withstand. "Why rebuild ancient walls?" is a question offered to trip the neighbor. But one of the surprises in "Mending Wall" is that the neighbor responds with a defense. He does not fall forward. He cannot be tripped into darkness—and a new outlook. Instead, threatened, he reaches into the past for support and comes up with his father's proverb: "Good fences make good neighbors." When we fail to recognize that the neighbor replies to the poet's prodding with a *proverb*, we miss a good deal of Frost's point.

Current in America as early as 1850, "Good fences make good neighbors" can be traced to the Spanish, "Una pared entre dos vezinos guarda más (haze durar) la amistad," which goes back at least to the Middle Ages.[12] In this form, Vicesimus Knox translated it for his compendium of *Elegant Extracts* in 1797, and in 1832 Emerson recorded it in his journal—"A wall between both, best preserves friendship."[13] That Frost encountered the idea in Emerson's published journals is probable, though it seems more likely that he found its precise expression elsewhere. For our purpose it is important that both Frost and Emerson were attracted to the same idea, suggesting an affinity of poetic temperament. "The sea, vocation, poverty, are seeming fences, but man is insular and cannot be touched."[14] In sentiment this is vintage Frost, but Emerson made the remark.

Speech in proverbial form surfaces as the poem's final "wall." Since the proverb's message is sanctioned by tradition, the poet's neighbor can retreat to safety. Resorting to a proverb enables him, moreover, to have the last word in the exchange. The importance of what he chooses to say is exceeded by the import of *how* he has chosen to say it. Provoked into speech, the farmer hides behind a clinching proverb. Twice the proverb is offered to close the matter. Failing to understand the message the first time, the poet repeats his question. The neighbor employs his proverb to win his point, even as it is employed in some African tribes, for example, where participants are allowed to use proverbs in litigation.[15]

What finally emerges from Frost's poem is the idea that the stock reply—unexamined wisdom from the past—seals off the possibility of further thought and communication. When thought has frozen into folk expression, language itself becomes another wall, one unresponsive to that which it encircles and given over to fulfilling a new and perhaps unintended function. Meeting once a year and insulated from anything beyond simple interaction by their well-defined duties and limits, these "good" neighbors turn out to be almost incommunicative.

It is difficult to ascertain Frost's full intent in linking "Mending Wall" with "The Tuft of Flowers." If the latter is about unexpected fellowship, then some interesting possibilities present themselves when it is paired with "Mending Wall." One way of stating the theme of "The Tuft of Flowers" is that even when a man works alone he works with others—but that is hardly the theme of "Mending Wall." On the contrary, in "Mending Wall" the poet discovers that, even when men work together, each of them works alone. "The Tuft of Flowers" also says that there can be communication without words, beyond physical presence and across time. But in "Mending Wall" we see that communication breaks down even as men converse. For Frost, "taking up a theme" did not at all entail dealing with it always in the same way. When we examine these linked poems in the light that each casts on the other, we find that their relationship really involves statement and counterstatement, or, put another way, theme and antitheme.

Yet if Frost could provide links between and among his poems to encourage the kind of cross-reading that he so much favored for poetry, he could also omit from his poems the kinds of links—in the form of pieces of information—that would show

him plainly to be writing in many cases within a larger histor-
ical and mythic context. Such is the case with "Mending Wall,"
in which the poet deliberately withholds a piece of useful infor-
mation.

"Who are bad neighbors?" asked Thoreau, for the sole pur-
pose of answering his own question. "They who suffer their
neighbors' cattle to go at large because they don't want their ill
will,—are afraid to anger them. They are abettors of the ill-
doers."[16] Thoreau could as readily have asked, "Who are good
neighbors?" Whereupon, following his reasoning, he could have
answered, "Those who build and maintain walls which keep out
their neighbors' cattle."

How, and indeed whether, the goodwill of one's neighbor is
fostered by boundaries, however, was a general question that
engaged Frost. Were walls and fences instrumental in the reten-
tion and renewal of human relationships? The answers pre-
sented in "Mending Wall" are somewhat less than clear-cut.
The reason is at least partly that Frost has purposely and pur-
posefully left out of his poem some important information. One
key to the poet's omission lies in the final lines of the poem.

> I see him there,
> Bringing a stone grasped firmly by the top
> In each hand, like an old-stone savage armed.
> He moves in darkness as it seems to me,
> Not of woods only and the shade of trees.
> He will not go behind his father's saying,
> And he likes having thought of it so well
> He says again, 'Good fences make good neighbors.'

In these lines the poet moves back through time, no longer
questioning the possible reasons for continuing annually to
repair the now apparently useless boundaries, and returns to an
earlier, darker age. Indeed, his neighbor seems to be moving in a
"darkness" that is, suggestively, "not of woods only and the
shade of trees." To the poet he is now "like an old-stone savage
armed." Even on New England farms in this century the ways of
the savage continue, it would seem, no matter how transformed
they may be or how radically attenuated.

Indeed, Frost shrewdly and characteristically stopped his

poem just short of a mythological link. That Frost and his neighbor engage in what is tantamount to a vestigial ritual and that, furthermore, prodded by the poet, the neighbor would defend his father's idea (proverbially expressed)[17] that "Good fences make good neighbors" relates this poem to traditions and rituals antedating the Romans. The god of boundaries they named Terminus was not invented by the Romans, but he became one of their important household gods.[18] Terminus was annually honored in a ritual that not only reaffirmed boundaries but also provided the occasion for predetermined traditional festivities among neighbors.

The festival of the *Terminalia* was celebrated in Rome and in the country on the 23rd of February. The neighbours on either side of any boundary gathered round the landmark [the stones which marked boundaries], with their wives, children, and servants; and crowned it, each on his own side, with garlands, and offered cakes and bloodless sacrifices. In later times, however, a lamb, or sucking pig, was sometimes slain, and the stone sprinkled with the blood. Lastly, the whole neighbourhood joined in a general feast.[19]

If the poet's neighbor does not know that this annual ritual of walking the boundaries to repair their common wall has its obscure source in the all but totally lost mysteries of ancient man, that information could not possibly have been unknown to the serious student of the classics who wrote the poem and who had read in *Walden* of Thoreau's search for firewood: "An old forest fence which had seen its best days was a great haul for me. I sacrificed it to Vulcan, for it was past serving the god Terminus."[20] What impresses itself on Frost, however, is something quite different. Whatever the reason, men continue to need marked boundaries, even when they find it difficult to justify their existence.

FOURTEEN

Dominion

Why level downward to our dullest perception always, and
praise that as common sense?
—Henry David Thoreau, *Walden* (1854)

JUST BEFORE its publication in 1936, Frost wrote
that his latest collection *A Further Range* might well "shock"
his readers for its "novelty."[1] As things turned out, the volume
shocked its readers less than it gave them fresh evidence of the
author's poetic prowess. In fact, it brought forth several poems
that would enter Frost's canon, including "Two Tramps in Mud
Time," "On the Heart's Beginning to Cloud the Mind," and "A
Drumlin Woodchuck," as well as two of his most popular
"insect" poems, "Departmental" and "The White-Tailed Hor-
net." Both of these typically Frostian poems could have been
furnished with an appropriate epigraph from Emerson's *Nature*,
but "Departmental" seems to fit more closely: "The instincts
of the ant are very unimportant considered as the ant's; but the
moment a ray of relation is seen to extend from it to man, and
the little drudge is seen to be a monitor, a little body with a
mighty heart, then all its habits, even that said to be recently
observed, that it never sleeps, become sublime."[2] "Departmen-
tal" takes up the organized rigamarole in the ant world imme-
diately subsequent to the death of the speaker's "Ant Jerry."

Laid out in heroic couplets, "Departmental" satirizes plan-
ners, organizers, and social engineers. The poem is a mock epic
harking back to Swift and Pope. It might appropriately have
been called, with a double sense, "The Antiad"; after all, Ant
Jerry, dead, is carried off the battlefield we name life.

"Departmental" tells us that, whether we discover in the

ways of the ant a desirable paradigm for human social organiza-
tion or whether we merely project upon the patterns of insect
behavior our own human web of interpretation, there remains
something utterly inhuman about such thinking. Man must not
be too ready to discover his truths and values, large and small, in
the ways of the insect world even as he must not throw the pall
of his human concerns and values over an insect world in which
those concerns and values do not inhere. Decidedly a skeptical
moralist's poem, "Departmental" lays waste all notions such as
the one just quoted from Emerson. Here is a theory, Frost seems
to say, that greatly needs revision.

The same need to revise theories applies in the case of "The
White-Tailed Hornet." This poem takes as its target fashionable
(and rather facile) notions on evolution, such as the evolution or
devolution (the literary perversion of Darwin) of man from the
"monkey" (see Frost's "The Literate Farmer and the Planet
Venus")—or so one might interpret the poet's attack in "The
White-Tailed Hornet" on those who make "downward com-
parisons."[3] But Frost's attack is subtler than bald criticism of
Darwinism. Actually, it is more reasonable to consider playing
off "The White-Tailed Hornet" against other, more specific
texts: the Psalms, William James, Emerson, and J. Henri Fabre.
Verses 4-8 of Psalm 8 make up the first text:

What is man, that thou art mindful of him? and the son of man, that
thou visitest him?

For thou hast made him a little lower than the angels, and hast crowned
him with glory and honour.

Thou madest him to have dominion over the works of thy hands; thou
hast put all things under his feet:

All sheep and oxen, yea, and the beasts of the field;

The fowl of the air, and the fish of the sea, and whatsoever passeth
through the paths of the seas.

William James, in his lectures on pragmatism, affirmed that
man stands somewhere above the animals and below the angels,

though he omitted mention of the angels. "I firmly disbelieve, myself," he wrote,

> that our human experience is the highest form of experience extant in the universe. I believe rather that we stand in much the same relation to the whole of the universe as our canine and feline pets do to the whole of human life. They inhabit our drawing-rooms and libraries. They take part in scenes of whose significance they have no inkling. They are merely tangent to curves of history the beginnings and ends and forms of which pass wholly beyond their ken. So we are tangent to the wider life of things. But, just as many of the dog's and cat's ideals coincide with our ideals, and the dogs and cats have daily living proof of the fact, so we may well believe, on the proofs that religious experience affords, that higher powers exist and are at work to save the world on ideal lines similar to our own.[4]

James, of course, wanted to make it painfully clear in this lecture on "Pragmatism and Religion" that his own pragmatism could not be charged with being an atheistic system.

That "The White-Tailed Hornet" also reminds us of man's scriptural dominion over the beasts, the fowl, and the fish is evident when the poet echoes Psalm 8:5 in the lines:

> As long on earth
> As our comparisons were stoutly upward
> With gods and angels, we were men at least,
> But little lower than the gods and angels.

Emerson, in his essay "The Comic," also distinguishes between man and those other creatures: "With the trifling exception of the stratagems of a few beasts and birds, there is no seeming, no halfness in Nature, until the appearance of man. Unconscious creatures do the whole will of wisdom. An oak or a chestnut undertakes no function it cannot execute. . . . The same rule holds true of the animals. Their activity is marked by unerring good sense."[5] Frost undoubtedly shares Emerson's notion (and the Bible's) that the existing clear-cut distinctions between man and the animals make all the difference. "God defend me," wrote Emerson on another occasion, "from ever looking at man as an animal."[6] No quarrel in that, certainly, between Frost and Emerson. But the notion (shared by Emerson) that animal activity is "marked by unerring good sense" (by which Emerson suggests that animals possess an unfailing instinct) is the primary butt of Frost's entire poem. Frost describes the white-tailed hornet's mock-epic adventures as it hunts its prey:

> I watched him where he swooped, he pounced, he struck;
> But what he found he had was just a nailhead.
> He struck a second time. Another nailhead.
> 'Those are just nailheads. Those are fastened down.'
> Then disconcerted and not unannoyed,
> He stooped and struck a little huckleberry
> The way a player curls around a football.
> 'Wrong shape, wrong color, and wrong scent,' I said.
> The huckleberry rolled him on his head.
> At last it was a fly. He shot and missed;
> And the fly circled round him in derision.
> But for the fly he might have made me think
> He had been at his poetry, comparing
> Nailhead with fly and fly with huckleberry:
> How like a fly, how very like a fly.
> But the real fly he missed would never do,
> The missed fly made me dangerously skeptic.

—skeptical of theories, that is, both his own and those of others—

> Won't this whole instinct matter bear revision?
> Won't almost any theory bear revision?
> To err is human, not to, animal.
> Or so we pay the compliment to instinct,
> Only too liberal of our compliment
> That really takes away instead of gives.

At this point the poet's complaint echoes that of Fabre (whom Maeterlinck called "the Homer of insects"): "To disparage man and exalt animals in order to establish a point of contact, followed by a point of union, has been and still is the general tendency of the 'advanced theories' in fashion in our day."[7] To be

sure, Fabre observed as much after having concluded that, in a
case involving a Wasp's operation with a Fly, "far from seeing the
least sign of reason in this, I look upon it as a mere act of
instinct, one so elementary that it is really not worth expatiat-
ing upon."[8] But while Frost agrees with Fabre that instinct and
not reason is operative in the actions of wasps, hornets, and
other insects, he takes issue with the Fabre who throughout his
work discovers conclusive evidence to establish the "over-
whelming superiority" of instinct over reasoning power.[9] His
works are paeans to that superiority: "O wonderful power of
instinct!"[10] The poet impugns the hapless hornet's powers of
instinct, its eyesight, and its memory.[11] The hornet makes
mistake after mistake, each time failing to learn from experi-
ence (this behavior accords with Fabre's statements). The poet
comments, somewhat tongue in cheek, that, because of the
hornet's abject failures that day, "Nothing but fallibility was left
us" (that is, to human beings), "And this day's work made even
that seem doubtful." In this light the poet constructs his first
"theory" that the hornet does not really make mistakes but is
actually working away at its poetry: the discovery of metaphor
and the making of a simile. But when it misses the "real" fly, the
game is up. Fabre had written confidently that "in the uncon-
scious inspiration of her instinct the Wasp has all the resources
of consummate art."[12] Maybe this statement held true for
Fabre's wasp, but it is patently untrue of Frost's hornet.

Given the hornet's string of failures, it is no wonder the poet
will consider revising his notions about the infallibility of an
insect's instinct and man's evolution, also questioning com-
parisons that are no longer "stoutly upward / With gods and
angels" but are "yielded downward":

> Once we began to see our images
> Reflected in the mud and even dust,
> 'Twas disillusion upon disillusion.
> We were lost piecemeal to the animals,
> Like people thrown out to delay the wolves.

Frost put his attack on the latest evolutionary theories dif-
ferently in another poem. In "The Literate Farmer and the

Planet Venus," the poet starts out with a reference to Thomas Edison and his great invention and ends sardonically with an appeal to scripture:

> It's a new patented electric light,
> Put up on trial by that Jerseyite
> So much is being now expected of,
> To give developments the final shove
> And turn us into the next specie folks
> Are going to be, unless these monkey jokes
> Of the last fifty years are all a libel,
> And Darwin's proved mistaken, not the Bible.[13]

As Frost said in his New Year's Day letter for 1917, "What I like about Bergson and Fabre is that they have bothered our evolutionism so much with the cases of instinct they have brought up."[14] But of course Frost soon found it necessary, as we have seen, to confound Bergson's and especially Fabre's notions on the infallibility of instinct with cases of his own that demonstrated the fallibility of the insect's instincts. The very subtitle of "The White-Tailed Hornet"—"The Revision of Theories"—hinted at his intentions.

Emerson's notion that man's appearance brought "halfness" to Nature, combined with the scriptural idea that "man is a little lower than the angels" (and in his own poem, he is "little lower than the gods and angels"), emerges surprisingly in a poem in which the poet, not deigning to explain the ways of man to God, merely indicates what to expect. For when God addresses him, the poet will not be there—by a half:

> I turned to speak to God
> About the world's despair;
> But to make bad matters worse
> I found God wasn't there.
>
> God turned to speak to me
> (Don't anybody laugh)
> God found I wasn't there—
> At least not over half.[15]

Surely, man's peculiar estate—this natural "halfness or imperfection"[16]—coupled with the other halfness that places him
a "little lower than the gods and angels"—contributes mightily
to the joke that God has played on man:

> Forgive, O Lord, my little jokes on Thee
> And I'll forgive Thy great big one on me.[17]

What little jokes, then, might man play in small-scale retaliation? His poetry—perhaps man's ability to compose poetry,
especially poems such as these. As Emerson had observed, the
"vitiating" of the "religious sentiment" results in "the joke of
jokes."[18] Indeed, he might have been explaining Frost's own
lines on God's and man's jokes when he wrote: "the relation of
the parties is inverted,"[19] that is, the man who, orthodoxically,
requires forgiveness has put to the Lord a proposition in which
he sets the conditions for a tradeoff (quid pro quo) of forgiveness.
Here, then, is Frost's version of the "joke of jokes" among those
countless jokes of jokes at the expense of the religious sentiment. Yet it is a joke that almost presupposes a fact about God.
The basis for his existence, if we are to judge from Frost's poems,
is that of James, who wrote, with no tolerance for nonsense:
"On pragmatistic principles, if the hypothesis of God works
satisfactorily in the widest sense of the word, it is true."[20] It was
particularly true, it seems, in "The Demiurge's Laugh," an early
poem in which Frost confesses embarrassment. The poet tells of
pursuing "the Demon's trail" well into "the sameness of the
wood," knowing he is after "no true god" and being stopped
short:

> The sound was behind me instead of before,
>   A sleepy sound, but mocking half,
> As of one who utterly couldn't care.
>   The Demon arose from his wallow to laugh[.]
> . . . .
> I shall not forget how his laugh rang out.
>   I felt as a fool to have been so caught,
> And checked my steps to make pretense
>   It was something among the leaves I sought[.][21]

It was "no true god" he found (and, conversely, no true god found him), but it was a god nevertheless, one who recalls the poet to his human's state of Emersonian halfness by laughing at him: "a sleepy sound, but mocking half." Only later, as we have seen, did the poet turn the tables.

FIFTEEN

Substantiation

A Word made Flesh is seldom
And tremblingly partook
Nor then perhaps reported
But have I not mistook
Each one of us has tasted
With ecstasies of stealth
The very food debated
To our specific strength—

A Word that breathes distinctly
Has not the power to die
Cohesive as the Spirit
It may expire if He—
"Made Flesh and dwelt among us"
Could condescension be
Like this consent of Language
This loved Philology.
—Emily Dickinson (date unknown)

WITH FULL PROPRIETY, on the occasion of his receipt of the Emerson-Thoreau Medal in 1959 from the American Academy of Arts and Sciences, Frost insisted that he was there "out of admiration for Emerson and Thoreau.[1] His subject that day was to be Emerson, and he intended to make himself on that "proud occasion" "as much of an Emersonian" as he could.[2]

Frost's brief talk that evening is a storehouse of self-revealing perceptions and teasing observations. He returns to certain lines in Emerson's poem "Brahma" that had long baffled him and explains how he finally came to understand the poet's elusive meaning. "It is a long story of many experiences that let

me into the secret of: But thou, meek lover of the good! / Find
me, and turn thy back on heaven."

What baffled me was the Christianity in "meek lover of the good." I
don't like obscurity and obfuscation, but I do like dark sayings I must
leave the clearing of to time. And I don't want to be robbed of the
pleasure of fathoming depths for myself. It was a moment for me when I
saw how Shakespeare set bounds to science when he brought in the
North Star, "whose worth's unknown although his height be taken." Of
untold worth: it brings home some that should and some that shouldn't
come.[3]

In this passage, he already hints at a link between the title of his
final book of poems, *In the Clearing*, and "The Pasture," first
published in *North of Boston* and since 1923 the poem that he
had placed first in the various editions of his "selected" and
"complete" poems. In "The Pasture" the farmer-poet had ex-
tended a warm invitation (to his companion? to his lover? to his
reader?) to accompany him while he went out "to clean the
pasture spring . . . and wait to watch the water clear."[4] In the
book he published within a year of his death, he chose to lead off
the first of the book's three parts, also titled "In the Clearing,"
with the line "And wait to watch the water clear, I may" as an
epigraph. (He provided no epigraphs for the other two sections of
the book, "Cluster of Faith" and "Quandary.")

Frost also chose to employ an epigraph for the book as a
whole, though he called it a "frontispiece." He took lines from
his own poem, "Kitty Hawk," published later in the volume in
the section of poems gathered under the rubric "Cluster of
Faith."

> But God's own descent
> Into flesh was meant
> As a demonstration
> That the supreme merit
> Lay in risking spirit
> In substantiation.
> Spirit enters flesh
> And for all it's worth
> Charges into earth
> In birth after birth

Ever fresh and fresh.
We may take the view
That its derring-do
Thought of in the large
Is one mighty charge
On our human part
Of the soul's ethereal
Into the material.[5]

Frost's placement of these lines, extracted from what might at first glance appear to be largely a patriotic poem celebrating the invention of the airplane, gives them undeniable significance. Frost chose to link "substantiation" with Emerson's notion of it, giving his lines, oddly, a New England basis. In *Nature* Emerson had said simply, almost off-handedly, "there seems to be a necessity in spirit to manifest itself in material forms."[6] Frost made his link with Emerson visible when, in his speech before the American Academy of Arts and Sciences, he observed ironically:

Emerson was a Unitarian because he was too rational to be superstitious and too little a storyteller and lover of stories to like gossip and pretty scandal. Nothing very religious can be done for people lacking in superstition. They usually end up abominable agnostics. It takes superstition and the prettiest scandal story of all to make a good Trinitarian. It is the first step in the descent of the spirit into the material-human at the risk of the spirit.[7]

The key to understanding Frost's in-school "fooling" is the word "superstitious." Of course, Emerson was superstitious (and so too was Frost) in the sense of the Latin *superstare*: to stand over, to dominate (especially in the face of the dominant beliefs—in our case, scientific—of our Western civilization). Awe before the "fact" of substantiation is a manifestation of superstition understood as Frost understood it.

The links that Frost identifies between his kind of superstition and poetry, as forces to be thrown up against the rationalism of science, he accounted for on another (and private) occasion:

You don't catch me walking into open competition with science in a scientific age—not unless science will promise me a return engagement in the next ensuing poetic age, which I predict will occur when as a final test of autonomy the Robot is called on in public to write good poetry and breaks down in tears admitting that he can't write very good—he can only write pretty good. You mark my word the final test of science is going to be what the synthetic man can do. All poetry is being kept alive for is to see if he can write it. He probably can—and will. But it will be something to be said for poetry that it was thought of as the highest proof of the Robot's arrival.[8]

Frost's talk on Emerson concludes with tributes to Washington (one of his "four greatest Americans") and, pertinently, to Emerson (another of his "greatest Americans"—the other two were Jefferson and Lincoln). This paragraph succeeds that which I have already quoted, on substantiation. "If Emerson had left us nothing else he would be remembered longer than the Washington Monument for the monument at Concord that he glorified with lines surpassing any other ever written about soldiers," writes Frost.[9] He then quotes the first stanza of "The Concord Hymn," Emerson's great poem, which in its entirety reads:

> By the rude bridge that arched the flood,
> Their flag to April's breeze unfurled,
> Here once the embattled farmers stood
> And fired the shot heard round the world.
>
> The foe long since in silence slept;
> Alike the conqueror silent sleeps;
> And Time the ruined bridge has swept
> Down the dark stream which seaward creeps.
>
> On this green bank, by this soft stream,
> We set to-day a votive stone;
> That memory may their deed redeem,
> When, like our sires, our sons are gone.
>
> Spirit, that made those heroes dare
> To die, and leave their children free,
> Bid Time and Nature gently spare
> The shaft we raise to them and thee.[10]

"Not even Thermopylae has been celebrated better," concludes Frost, than by this "poem on stone."[11]

Frost could see himself as one of those embattled farmers who had also been at their own clarifying poetry, trying to make their gunshots speak of freedom. Earlier in his talk Frost had said that "freedom is nothing but departure—setting forth—leaving things behind, brave origination of the courage to be new. . . . Emerson supplies the emancipating formula for giving an attachment up for an attraction," insists Frost, "one nationality for another nationality, one love for another love."[12] The farmers' assertion of freedom is in itself an act of Emersonian poetry; they left off being farmers to become for the time needful soldiers, giving up their attachment to one nation for a new attraction. This rebellion is now commemorated both in Emerson's own deed—the poem (Frost defined poetry as "words that have become deeds")[13]—and in the monument that carries his lines of clarification chiseled into its stone.

It is of considerable interest that when Frost wrote his own lines clarifying the theme of the soldier—"What's worth living for is worth dying for"[14]—he chose to echo Emerson's celebratory poem. Frost collected "A Soldier" in *West-Running Brook* (1928):

> Here is that fallen lance that lies as hurled,
> That lies unlifted now, come dew, come rust,
> But still lies pointed as it plowed the dust.
> If we who sight along it round the world,
> See nothing worthy to have been its mark,
> It is because like men we look too near,
> Forgetting that as fitted to the sphere,
> Our missiles always make too short an arc.
> They fall, they rip the grass, they intersect
> The curve of earth, and striking, break their own;
> They make us cringe for metal-point on stone.
> But this we know, the obstacle that checked
> And tripped the body, shot the spirit on
> Further than target ever showed or shone.[15]

Boldly Frost reemploys Emerson's exceedingly familiar phrase "round the world" in his own salute to the fallen soldier, and in conclusion he echoes Emerson's own concluding apostrophe to "Spirit." But Emerson's soldier-farmers are also recalled in Frost's metaphor "plowed the dust." Interestingly, in "The Divinity School Address," Emerson, noting that the name of Jesus was "not so much written as ploughed into the history of this world," insisted: "One man was true to what is in you and me. He [Jesus] saw that God incarnates himself in man, and evermore goes forth anew to take possession of his world."[16]

Such fervent stands on behalf of man and his freedom, and deaths suffered on behalf of freedom, Frost saw as deeds embodying the belief that it is worthwhile to abandon one thing for another, giving up one task in favor of turning to a fresh task. They served to remind Frost of his own imperative as a poet: "getting sharp, pointed meaning into the material."[17] Emerson had said, "American life storms about us daily, and is slow to find a tongue. This contemporary insight is transubstantiation, the conversion of daily bread into the holiest of symbols."[18] In a fallen world the poet's task was simply, as Frost saw things, to make flesh say spirit.

PART FOUR

Coda

SIXTEEN

Tributaries

There is nothing quite so composing as composition.
Putting anything in order [—] a house[,] a business[,] a
poem [—] gives a sense of sharing the mastery of the
universe.
—Robert Frost, undated (*Prose Jottings*, 1982)

WHEN FROST SPOKE at the Browne and Nichols
School on March 13, 1918, we should recall, his theme was "the
unmade word, or fetching and far-fetching."[1] As a poet, he
insisted, he had a predilection for "a figurative fetching of fresh
words" for his own use. He added: "The word lies in our every-
day speech, practical, hard, and unliterary; and that's the way I
like the word—there's where my fun with it begins. I don't care
for the word already made figurative." If it is clear that Frost
believes the poet has a duty to take the language of ordinary,
quotidian speech and make it figurative, interestingly enough,
he does not then as a poet feel obliged to indicate how he himself
has made such a transformation. The teacher in him prompts
him to show how someone else has failed to effect the poetic
miracle of making an everyday word his own.

Frost recalls the words that another teacher had spoken the
day before. "Inspired by the brilliant effect of the ice encased
trees, reflecting the morning in prismatic colors," begins the
poet-teacher,

he strove to add a new word to your vocabulary by quoting the opening
sentence of Emerson's famous Divinity School Address: "In this *re-
fulgent* summer it has been a luxury to draw the breath of life." Of
course, anybody would sit up and take notice when a speaker began like
that. Undoubtedly there's a freshness there in the use of that word that

amounts to brilliance; but you ought not to use the word in just that way.

His colleague's problem, as Frost saw it, was that the success of Emerson's figurative use of the word "refulgent" had made the word his. Emerson's success led Frost to advise leaving it alone.

In this instance, struck by the example of his fellow teacher, Frost followed his own advice. Nowhere in his published poetry does he employ the latinate term. But Browne was not alone among Frost's acquaintances in making the attempt to replicate Emerson's figurative use of "refulgent." Emerson's Concord neighbor Thoreau had slipped the term into the culminating last line of his fine poem, "Smoke in Winter": "And now, perchance, high in the crispy air, / [The smoke] has caught sight of the day o'er the earth's edge, / And greets its master's eye at his low door, / As some refulgent cloud in the upper sky."[2] Thoreau had not only employed the term Emerson had used so effectively to introduce his talk about a bright, shining, resplendent summer but had outdone Emerson by employing the word with great precision, convincing us that the word exactly describes this smoke which makes its way up into the atmosphere and toward the sun. This smoke cloud is appropriately refulgent not merely because it shines brightly but because it flashes back (from the Latin: *re*, "again, back," and *fulgeo*, "to shine"). Here, then, is Poetry enacted.

"Poetry is a prowess," wrote Frost in his notebooks and then added, "Poetry is the renewal of words."[3] True enough. But surely the function of Poetry, as Frost practiced it, was not limited to the renewal of words. If the truth were known, and Frost knew the truth, the composition of poetry was itself a form of renewal. It was neither accidental nor casual that Frost after 1923, it will be recalled, chose to lead off each of his volumes of complete poems with "The Pasture," which celebrates seasonal and personal renewal.

> I'm going out to clean the pasture spring;
> I'll only stop to rake the leaves away
> (and wait to watch the water clear, I may):
> I sha'n't be gone long.—You come too.

> I'm going out to fetch the little calf
> That's standing by the mother. It's so young
> It totters when she licks it with her tongue.
> I sha'n't be gone long.—You come too.[4]

With a nod in the direction of traditional pastoral lyrics (familiar to English-language readers from Marlowe's "Come with me and be my love"), Frost's speaker reenacts in one act of seasonal necessity Thoreau's emblematic journey to the outskirts of Concord. Just as Thoreau went to Walden Pond, so too does Frost's New England farmer return seasonally to his own pasture spring. No matter that it is just the pasture spring and that seemingly all the farmer-poet will derive from it (apart from its considerable usefulness for his cows) is the experience of watching "the water clear." Yet for a poet who would call his final book of poems and one published in the last year of his life *In the Clearing,* there can be no overemphasizing the import of so prominently and so consistently featuring "The Pasture." Clarity was of the essence, and with it came order—that stay against confusion. He put the same matter more aggressively in an even shorter poem. Recalling the Thoreau of "Smoke in Winter," Frost shouts in "Pertinax":

> Let chaos storm!
> Let cloud shapes swarm!
> I wait for form.[5]

This Frostian stridence, typical though it is, does not, however, tell the entire story. If this poet confidently awaited the emergence of form, he was also the poet who could say, with impatience, as he has Job say in *A Masque of Reason*: "The artist in me cries out for design."[6] In less heated moments, he might say, as the speaker does in the late poem "Accidentally on Purpose," "Grant me intention, purpose, and design— / That's near enough for me to the Divine."[7] And if the design is the one revealed in the sonnet he entitles "Design," what of that? Yes, even that design contributes to the whole, though the way it does might well be beyond man's knowing. For his principle is that "if there is a big design beyond us it is made out of the little

designs within our powers, not out of the general confusion. The
big aim is made out of our small aims of our concentrated
moments."[8] Yet as he noted on still another occasion, "a poem
is not a string but a web."[9]

If there was one major design (to turn from notions of pur-
pose to those of form) that linked Frost with his predecessors of
the New England Renaissance—that is, with Emerson, Thor-
eau, and Dickinson—it was inherent in the curve or circle.
There are paths leading back from Frost to the dazzling figu-
rative display that is Emerson's essay "Circles," the "magic
circle" of *Walden*, and the cluster of Dickinson poems in which
she investigates circles and circumference and in the course of
which she discovers the "Circuit" of "Truth." Frost was fasci-
nated with curves, circles, concentrations, and circulation. Re-
peatedly, as Frost thinks aloud, we come upon notions of circu-
larity. His notes and poems include pertinent observations such
as these:

1. All reasoning is in a circle[,] I say. At any rate[,] all learning is in a
circle. We learn A[,] the better to learn B[,] the better to learn C[,] the
better to learn D[,] the better to learn A. All we get of A is enough to
start us on the way to take it up later again. We should circulate among
the facts[,] not progress through them leaving some forever behind[.][10]

2. And then there are circular runs[,] like the stone[,] the knife[,] the
handkerchief of the Japanese game. The stone is better than the knife
because it can dull the knife, the knife is better than the handkerchief
becau[s]e it can cut the handkerchief. The handkerchief is better than
the stone because it can cover the stone. . . . Nowhere can man seem to
check himself in these circulations. . . . The mind of man is an un-
vicious circle that no desperation can break through. Knowledge is the
same. We get a slight hold on our first poem the better to understand
our second, the better still our third[,] and so on till we are back[,] with
all our experience of poetry[,] on a day the better to understand our first
poem.[11]

3. Space is said to be circular. I don't know whether it is or not. I
suspect the curviture of the mind[,] which makes us reason always in a
circle[,] would make the universe look curved even in its straightest
lines. Some telescope will be strong enough for us to look at our own
back hair.[12]

4. The serpent's tail stuck down the serpent's throat,

> Which is the symbol of eternity
> And also of the way all things come round,
> Or of how rays return upon themselves,
> To quote the greatest Western poem yet.[13]

We can stop with these quotations to focus briefly on the fourth one, lines from the dramatic poem *A Masque of Reason* (1945). The encomium to "the greatest Western poem yet," as Frost's informed readers have long known, refers to Emerson's "Uriel," the salient lines of which for Frost's purposes are "Line in nature is not found; / Unit and universe are round; / In vain produced, all rays return; / 'Evil will bless, and ice will burn.' "[14] These lines from Emerson's poem—attending to the primacy of the metaphor of circularity and return (and Frost did believe that for man education comes through metaphor)—anticipate the truth in "Directive," of which the poet said, it will be recalled, that "the key lines . . . are 'Cold as a spring as yet so near its source, / Too lofty and original to rage,' " and that "the key word in the whole poem is source—whatever source it is."[15] "Source" keys as well into "West-Running Brook," the long, discursive poem in which Frost's speakers read an emblematic truth into the quirky behavior of a stream that at one point flows back on itself:

> Not just a swerving, but a throwing back,
> As if regret were in it and were sacred.
> It has this throwing backward on itself
> So that the fall of most of it is always
> Raising a little, sending up a little.
> Our life runs down in sending up the clock.
> The brook runs down in sending up our life.
> The sun runs down in sending up the brook.
> And there is something sending up the sun.
> It is this backward motion toward the source,
> Against the stream, that most we see ourselves in,
> The tribute of the current to the source.[16]

It is not far-fetched to see in this "tribute of the current to the source" an analogue for the kind of tribute Frost's fetching poems pay to his New England predecessors when he draws upon them for substance—thought, symbol, image, and language. In this respect, Frost was profoundly traditional, for he knew that his "new" poetry, its composition as well as the reading of it, depended on them. As he said, speaking for the maker as well as the reader, "The object of it all is to get among the poems where they throw light on each other."[17] Thus Frost the poet and reader pays his New Englander's tribute to the main sources and the local currents.

NOTES

Preface: RAKING THE LEAVES AWAY

1. Ralph Waldo Emerson, "Resources," in *Complete Works of Ralph Waldo Emerson* (Boston: Houghton Mifflin, 1903-1904), vol. 8: *Letters and Social Aims*, pp. 151-52.

2. *Robert Frost: Farmer-Poultryman*, ed. Edward Connery Lathem and Lawrance Thompson (Hanover, N.H.: Dartmouth Publications, 1963), p. 83.

3. See George Monteiro, "Frost's Quest for the 'Purple Fringed,'" *English Language Notes* 13 (March 1976): 204-6.

4. Quoted in Vrest Orton, *Vermont Afternoons with Robert Frost* (Rutland, Vt.: Charles E. Tuttle, 1971), p. 20.

5. Lawrance Thompson, *Robert Frost: The Early Years, 1874-1915* (New York: Holt, Rinehart and Winston, 1966).

6. John C. Kemp, *Robert Frost and New England: The Poet as Regionalist* (Princeton, N.J.: Princeton Univ. Press, 1979).

7. Ralph Waldo Emerson, "Quotation and Originality," in *Complete Works of Emerson*, vol. 8: *Letters and Social Aims*, p. 178.

8. "The Prerequisites," in *Selected Prose of Robert Frost*, ed. Hyde Cox and Edward Connery Lathem (New York: Holt, Rinehart and Winston, 1966), p. 97.

1. DIRECTIVES

1. "Directive," in *Complete Poems of Robert Frost, 1949* (New York: Henry Holt, 1949), pp. 520-21.

2. See S.P.C. Duvall, "Robert Frost's 'Directive' out of *Walden*," *American Literature* 31 (January 1960):482-88.

3. Quoted in Theodore Morrison, "The Agitated Heart," *Atlantic Monthly* 220 (July 1967): 79.

4. "The Over-Soul," in *Collected Works of Ralph Waldo Emerson*, vol. 2: *Essays, 1st Ser.*, introduced and annotated by Joseph Slater, text established by Alfred R. Ferguson and Jean Ferguson Carr (Cambridge, Mass.: Harvard Univ. Press, 1979), p. 159.

5. Elaine Barry, *Robert Frost on Writing* (New Brunswick, N.J.: Rutgers Univ. Press, 1973), p. 116.

6. "A Literary Dialogue," *Amherst Writing* 39 (May 1925):4.

7. Barry, *Frost on Writing*, p. 145.

8. Ibid.

9. Here Frost echoes Emerson, who, in "Quotation and Originality," warns: "We dislike that the poet should choose an antique or far-fetched subject for his muse" (*Complete Works of Emerson*, vol. 8: *Letters and Social Aims*, p. 203).

10. *Walden*, ed. J. Lyndon Shanley (Princeton, N.J.: Princeton Univ. Press, 1971), pp. 244-45.

11. Barry, *Frost on Writing*, p. 148.

12. Richard Wilbur, *Responses: Prose Pieces, 1953-1976* (New York: Harcourt Brace Jovanovich, 1976), p. 113.

13. Ibid., p. 111.

14. "The Prerequisites," p. 97.

15. "Poetry's Debt to Poetry," *Hudson Review* 26 (Summer 1973):292.

16. Quoted in Reginald L. Cook, "Robert Frost in Context," in *Frost: Centennial Essays III*, ed. Jac Tharpe (Jackson: Univ. Press of Mississippi, 1978), p. 139.

17. Quoted in Hyatt H. Waggoner, *American Poets: From the Puritans to the Present* (Boston: Houghton Mifflin, 1968), p. 324.

18. Quoted in Reginald Cook, *Robert Frost: A Living Voice* (Amherst: Univ. of Massachusetts Press, 1974), p. 144.

19. "Quotation and Originality," p. 194.

2. DANGLING CONVERSATION

1. Robert Hillyer, *A Letter to Robert Frost and Others* (New York: Knopf, 1937), p. 4.

2. Quoted in Louis Mertins, *Robert Frost: Life and Talks—Walking* (Norman: Univ. of Oklahoma Press, 1965), p. 385.

3. Reginald L. Cook, *The Dimensions of Robert Frost* (New York: Rinehart, 1958), pp. 56-57, 99; and Cook, *A Living Voice*, pp. 57, 243-44.

4. Daniel Smythe, *Robert Frost Speaks* (New York: Twayne, 1964), p. 140.

5. Cook, *Dimensions*, p. 56. See also *Frost: A Time to Talk: Conversations and Indiscretions Recorded by Robert Francis* (Amherst: Univ. of Massachusetts Press, 1972), pp. 53-54.

6. On dating Frost's discovery of Dickinson, see Thompson, *Early Years*, p. 124.

7. *Poems (1890-1896) by Emily Dickinson*, introduction by George Monteiro (Gainesville: Scholars' Facsimiles and Reprints, 1967), p. 134. Page numbers in my text below refer to this edition.

8. Susan Hayes Ward, the *Independent*'s literary editor, was pleased with "My Butterfly"—so much so, in fact, that five years after

its publication she gave its maker his first critical recognition in a national periodical: "Let me name here a few new writers whose work has not yet found much recognition. 'My Butterfly' (November 8th, 1894), which reads as if written with a practiced pen, was, I believe, the first poem its author, Robert Lee Frost, ever offered for publication. He was hardly past boyhood at the time, and the poem was written, he says, when it first dawned upon him that poetry 'ought to sound well'" ("A Decade of Poetry: 1889-1899," *Independent* 51 [September 28, 1899]: 2610-12).

    9. Thompson, *Early Years*, p. 162.

    10. In this respect Frost's poems go back to Dickinson's and through them to such earlier New England models as Emerson's "The Rhodora" and "Each and All," Longfellow's "Seaweed," and, even more pointedly, William Cullen Bryant's "To a Waterfowl."

    11. "Blue-Butterfly Day," in *Complete Poems, 1949*, p. 277.

    12. *Selected Letters of Robert Frost*, ed. Lawrance Thompson (New York: Holt, Rinehart and Winston, 1964), p. 45. Frost seems never to have assembled his "Moth and Butterfly" book.

    13. "Pod of the Milkweed," in *In the Clearing* (New York: Holt, Rinehart and Winston, 1962), pp. 13-14.

    14. Thompson, *Early Years*, p. 169.

    15. Ibid. When Frost submitted the poem to the *Independent* (49 [September 9, 1897]: 1161) he changed the pronoun in the last line from "she" to "he." Forty years later he admitted that he had made the change to "cover his tracks" (*Early Years*, p. 519).

    16. In *Early Years* (pp. 614, 169) Lawrance Thompson dates the composition of "Warning" to 1894 and the date of its transmission in manuscript to Elinor White as 1895, but later, in *Robert Frost: Poetry and Prose*, ed. Edward Connery Lathem and Lawrance Thompson (New York: Holt, Rinehart and Winston, 1972), p. 190, he gives 1895 as the date of composition. In both instances Thompson's conjectures are based on Frost's own not always reliable recollection on the occasion of the reprinting of "Warning" in *Three Poems* in 1935 (*Early Years*, p. 519). I would contest Frost's dating of the poem and would place the date close to the time of first publication (*Independent*, September 9, 1897).

    17. See Mertins, *Life and Talks—Walking*, p. 39, and *Interviews with Robert Frost*, ed. Edward Connery Lathem (New York: Holt, Rinehart and Winston, 1966), p. 230.

    18. "Revelation," in *Complete Poems, 1949*, p. 27.

    19. Lawrance Thompson, *Fire and Ice: The Art and Thought of Robert Frost* (New York: Holt, 1942), p. 131.

    20. "The Secret Sits," in *Complete Poems, 1949*, p. 495.

    21. Untitled, in *In the Clearing*, p. 39.

    22. In *Complete Poems, 1949*, pp. 458-59, "The Quest of the Orchis" is retitled "The Quest of the Purple-Fringed."

23. Thompson, *Early Years*, p. 218.
24. Mrs. William Starr Dana, *How to Know the Wild Flowers* (New York: Scribner's, 1893), p. 274.
25. Francis, *Frost: A Time to Talk*, p. 7.

3. ONE HAND CLAPPING

1. *Emily Dickinson: Three Views* (Amherst: Amherst College Press, 1960).
2. Mertins, *Life and Talks—Walking*, pp. 384-85.
3. Cook, *A Living Voice*.
4. Mertins, *Life and Talks—Walking*, p. 385.
5. *Interviews with Robert Frost*, p. 126.
6. Cook, *A Living Voice*, p. 157.
7. *Interviews with Robert Frost*, p. 238.
8. "A Mystical Poet," in *Emily Dickinson: Three Views*, pp. 33-34.
9. Cook, *A Living Voice*, p. 162.
10. Quoted in John S. Van E. Kohn, "Giving Emily Dickinson to the World," *Princeton University Library Quarterly* 31 (Autumn 1969): 48.
11. *The Letters of Robert Frost to Louis Untermeyer* (New York: Holt, Rinehart and Winston, 1963), p. 203.
12. Cook, *A Living Voice*, p. 57.
13. See Karl Keller, *The Only Kangaroo among the Beauty* (Baltimore: Johns Hopkins Univ. Press, 1979), pp. 312-13.
14. Cook, *Dimensions*, p. 56.
15. This "construction" of Frost's remarks derives from Smythe, *Robert Frost Speaks*, p. 140; Cook, *Dimensions*, pp. 56-57 and 99; Francis, *Frost: A Time to Talk*, pp. 53-54; Cook, *A Living Voice*, pp. 41, 51, 56, 57-58, and 111; Barry, *Frost on Writing*, pp. 62, 67, 68, 71-72, 121, 147-48, and 161; and *Complete Poems, 1949*, p. 149.

4. DESIGNS

1. "On the Relation of Man to the Globe," in *The Early Lectures of Ralph Waldo Emerson*, vol. 1: *1833-1836*, ed. Stephen E. Whicher and Robert E. Spiller (Cambridge, Mass.: Harvard Univ. Press, 1959), p. 49.
2. *Selected Letters of Robert Frost*, p. 45.
3. The "In White" manuscript, now at the Huntington Library, San Marino, California, was published first in Cook, *Dimensions*, p. 85. It was subsequently republished, with slight differences in transcription, in Thompson's *Early Years*, p. 582.
4. Cook, *Dimensions*, p. 85.
5. "Design," in *Complete Poems, 1949*, p. 396. Three commentaries on "Design" are indispensable: Randall Jarrell, *Poetry and the Age* (New York: Vintage, 1955), pp. 42-45; Reuben A. Brower, *The*

Poetry of Robert Frost: Constellations of Intention (New York: Oxford Univ. Press, 1963), pp. 103-8); and Waggoner, *American Poets*, p. 4 and *passim*.

6. See Brower, *Poetry of Robert Frost*, p. 105.

7. Thompson suggests that the lines "What brought the kindred spider to that height, / Then steered the white moth thither in the night?" are a mock-echo of the well-known lines of William Cullen Bryant's poem on providential design, "To a Waterfowl": "He, who, from zone to zone, / Guides through the boundless sky thy certain flight" (*Early Years*, p. 582).

8. Quoted in Cook, *A Living Voice*, p. 114. It is not without interest or significance that Emerson, in "Poetry and Imagination," writes animatedly: "Great design belongs to a poem. . . . We want design, and do not forgive the bards if they have only the art of enamelling. We want an architect, and they bring us an upholsterer. If your subject do not appear to you the flower of the world at this moment, you have not rightly chosen it. No matter what it is, grand or gay, national or private, if it has a natural prominence to you, work away until you come to the heart of it: then it will, though it were a sparrow or a spider-web, as fully represent the central law and draw all tragic or joyful illustration, as if it were the book of Genesis or the book of Doom" (*Complete Works of Emerson*, 8:33-34).

9. *National Poetry Festival: Held in the Library of Congress, October 22-24, 1962, Proceedings* (Washington, D.C.: Library of Congress, 1964), p. 234.

10. Elizabeth Shepley Sergeant, *Robert Frost: The Trial by Existence* (New York: Holt, Rinehart and Winston, 1960), p. 28. (See also Allan Houston Macdonald, *Richard Hovey: Man and Craftsman* [Durham, N.C.: Duke Univ. Press, 1957], p. 112, n. 113.) The *Independent*'s rather extravagant editorial ("Richard Hovey's Poem") read in part: "Mr. Hovey's elegy does not follow the classical example of Milton's 'Lycidas,' Shelley's 'Adonais,' and Arnold's 'Thyrsis,' three of the great elegies of the English language. It is modern and American. . . . [It] will, we think, be numbered among the great elegies of the language" (44:1626-27). No wonder the young Frost was pumped up, especially since he must have felt that he could write poetry as good, at least, as Hovey's.

11. "Design," *Independent* 44 (December 15, 1892): 1773.

12. "My Butterfly," *Independent* 46 (November 8, 1894):1429.

13. "From an American Sermon," *Independent* 44 (December 15, 1892):1773.

14. "My Butterfly," p. 1429.

15. For the argument that "Design" shows the influence of William James's *Pragmatism*, see Thompson, *Early Years*, pp. 383-87, and for a reading of the poem based on Thompson's suggestion, see Richard Poirier, *Robert Frost: The Work of Knowing* (New York: Oxford Univ. Press, 1977), pp. 245-52, 255-59. It is useful to note, however, that James

is possibly reacting to Emerson's lecture "On the Relation of Man to the Globe," specifically the passage quoted at the beginning of this chapter.

5. ROADS AND PATHS

1. See Samuel C. Chew, *The Pilgrimage of Life* (New Haven: Yale Univ. Press, 1962), pp. 175-81.
2. Ibid., p. 178.
3. *The Divine Comedy of Dante Alighieri*, trans. Henry Wadsworth Longfellow (Boston: Houghton Mifflin, 1895), p. 3.
4. "The Road Not Taken," in *Complete Poems, 1949*, p. 131.
5. Chew, *Pilgrimage of Life*, pp. 180-81.
6. Quoted in Philip L. Gerber, "Remembering Robert Frost: An Interview with William Jewell," *New England Quarterly* 59 (March 1986):21.
7. *The Divine Comedy of Dante Alighieri*, trans. Charles Eliot Norton, rev. ed., vol. 1: *Hell* (Boston: Houghton Mifflin, 1903), p. 1.
8. Sergeant, *Trial by Existence*, pp. 87-88.
9. Gerber, "Remembering Robert Frost," p. 21.
10. *Selected Letters of Robert Frost*, p. xiv.
11. Henry Wadsworth Longfellow, *Drift-Wood*, in *Outre-Mer and Drift-Wood* (Boston: Houghton Mifflin, 1886), pp. 405-6.
12. William James, "The Will to Believe," in *Pragmatism and Other Essays*, introduced by Joseph L. Blau (New York: Washington Square Press, 1963), p. 213.
13. *Poems (1890-1896) by Emily Dickinson*, p. 364.
14. "Stopping by Woods on a Snowy Evening," in *Complete Poems, 1949*, p. 275.
15. Norton, *Divine Comedy*, p. 1.
16. Longfellow, *Divine Comedy*, p. 3. In "conversation" Frost occasionally referred to the *Inferno*; see Cook, "Frost in Context," pp. 134, 138.
17. Quoted in Cook, *A Living Voice*, p. 81.
18. "The Draft Horse," in *In the Clearing*, p. 60.
19. Stephen Crane, *The Black Riders and Other Lines* (Boston: Copeland and Day, 1895), p. 62.
20. *A Masque of Mercy*, in *Complete Poems, 1949*, p. 632.

6. EDUCATION BY METAPHOR

1. Quoted in Charles W. Cole, "Metaphor and Syllogism," *Massachusetts Review* 4 (Winter 1963):241-42.
2. "A Parallel of Parablists: Thoreau and Frost," in *The Thoreau*

Centennial, ed. Walter Harding (New York: State Univ. of New York Press, 1964), pp. 65-79.

3. *Books We Like: Sixty-Two Answers,* preface by Edward Weeks (Boston: Massachusetts Library Association, 1936), p. 142.

4. Quoted in Sergeant, *Trial by Existence,* p. 191.

5. *Selected Letters of Robert Frost,* pp. 182, 278.

6. "Thoreau's *Walden:* Discussion between Robert Frost and Reginald Cook," introduced by J. Isaacs, *Listener* 52 (August 26, 1954):319-20; reprinted in *Interviews with Robert Frost,* pp. 142-47.

7. "Robert Frost on 'Extravagance,'" *Dartmouth Alumni Magazine* 55 (March 1963):21-24. This lecture is conveniently reprinted in *Robert Frost: Poetry and Prose,* pp. 447-59. For studies of Frost's specific debts to Thoreau, see Duvall, "Robert Frost's 'Directive' "; Daniel G. Hoffman, "Thoreau's 'Old Settler' and Frost's Paul Bunyan," *Journal of American Folklore* 73 (July-September 1960):236-38; George W. Nitchie, *Human Values in the Poetry of Robert Frost* (Durham, N.C.: Duke Univ. Press, 1960), pp. 19-20, 43, and passim; Thornton H. Parsons, "Thoreau, Frost, and the American Humanist Tradition," *Emerson Society Quarterly* (Fourth Quarter 1963): 33-43; Mario L. D'Avanzo, "How to Build a Chimney: Frost Gleans Thoreau," *Thoreau Journal Quarterly* 9 (October 1977): 24-26; Fred Durden, "Thoreau and Frost: Birds of a Feather," *Thoreau Journal Quarterly* 9 (October 1977): 28-32; Fritz Oehlschlaeger, "Two Woodchucks, or Frost and Thoreau on the Art of the Burrow," *Colby Library Quarterly* 18 (December 1982): 214-19; Barton Levi St. Armand, "Frost's 'Mending Wall,' " *Explicator* 41 (Fall 1982): 47-48. Less specific in their treatment of Frost's indebtedness to Thoreau but of central significance to anyone interested in the subject are the studies published by Cook, *Dimensions;* Brower, *Poetry of Robert Frost;* and Thompson, *Early Years.*

8. *Selected Letters of Robert Frost,* p. 182.

9. "Of Axe-Handles and Guide-Book Poetry," *Interviews with Robert Frost,* p. 19; first published in the *Public Ledger* (Phildelphia), April 4, 1916.

10. *Walden,* p. 144.

11. In *Walden* Thoreau chose not to give the name of his woodchopper, it may be recalled, even though his *Journals* reveal that it was Alek Therien. Faced with a similar choice, Frost decided to name his woodchopper. But why name him Baptiste? It may be speculated, reasonably I think, that Frost, making his Baptiste something of a wise fool, is drawing upon, and slyly manipulating, a familiar French-Canadian folk tradition. "In popular speech," observes Gerard J. Brault, "*Baptiste* is often used in addressing a child familiarly or as a humorous exclamation; in modern French patois it may designate a fool" ("Five Canadian-French Etymologies," *Romance Philology* 14 [August 1960]:20).

12. Published originally in *Atlantic Monthly* 120 (September 1917): 337-39, "The Ax-Helve" was collected by Frost in *New Hamp-*

shire: A Poem with Notes and Grace Notes (New York: Henry Holt, 1923), and later in *Complete Poems, 1949*. A comparison of these printings turns up only minor textual differences. I quote the poem exclusively from *Complete Poems, 1949*, pp. 228-31.

13. Attempts at creating natural form by the artificial means of machinery and instruments continued to plague Frost. For example, in his most famous essay, "The Figure a Poem Makes," he writes: "We enjoy the straight crookedness of a good walking stick. Modern instruments of precision are being used to make things crooked as if by eye and hand in the old days" (*Complete Poems, 1949*, p. vii).

14. *Selected Letters of Robert Frost*, p. 181.

15. Charles R. Anderson, "Robert Frost, 1874-1963," *Saturday Review*, February 23, 1963, p. 20.

16. *Selected Letters of Robert Frost*, p. 179.

17. Quoted in Reginald L. Cook, "Emerson and Frost: A Parallel of Seers," *New England Quarterly* 31 (June 1958):205. Italics added.

18. Quoted in Elizabeth Wahlquist, "You Don't Have to Go to Niagara to Write about Water: Robert Frost's Defense of Emily Dickinson," a paper presented at "Disclosures Toward Eternity: Emily Dickinson, 1830-1886: A Centennial Celebration," Brigham Young University, Provo, Utah, October 2, 1986.

7. BONFIRES

1. *Walden*, p. 251.

2. *The Blithedale Romance*, in *The Centenary Edition of Nathaniel Hawthorne*, 3 (Columbus: Ohio State Univ. Press, 1964): 211-12.

3. This fictional source for "The Wood-Pile" has been studied by Edward Stone, "Other 'Desert Places': Frost and Hawthorne," in *Frost: Centennial Essays*, compiled by the Committee on the Frost Centennial of the University of Southern Mississippi (Jackson: Univ. Press of Mississippi, 1974), pp. 282-83. In the same collection J. Donald Crowley locates Frost sources in several of Hawthorne's notebook entries ("Hawthorne and Frost: The Making of a Poem," pp. 288-309). The link between Hawthorne's novel and Frost's poem appears to have been made first by Alexander C. Kern, "Frost's 'The Wood-Pile,'" *Explicator* 28 (February 1970), item 49.

4. "The Wood-Pile," in *Complete Poems, 1949*, pp. 126-27.

5. *Walden*, p. 251.

6. The phrase "smokeless burning" offers us an interesting case of fetching by Frost. According to Reginald L. Cook, "The magic, Frost thought, was in the phrase 'smokeless burning.' It was, he added, one of 'the lucky snatches,' and he continued, elaborating felicitously, 'The magic of the thing is the lucky snatch you take as you go.' He had snatched it at the time from a firearms advertisement for smokeless

powder then in a current magazine. (*The Literary Digest* for August 25, 1906 on page 257 has an advertisement for Laflin and Rand's 'Infallible Smokeless' powder. The advertisement appears also in subsequent issues. But smokeless powder, no new thing, was of course first invented in 1863 by the German Schultze.) The phrase was 'the lucky snatch,' and, as Frost said about the things a writer picks up from here and there and uses in his own writing, he 'steals them to new uses.' Frost borrowed the firearm company's alluring phrase for a haunting line of poetry" ("Frost in Context," pp. 147-48).

7. Compare Frost's periodic use of similar phrases elsewhere: for example, in poems, "We turned to other things" ("The Exposed Nest") and "turned to their affairs" ("'Out, Out'—")—*Complete Poems, 1949*, pp. 137 and 172—and in conversation: "Had poetry been his only career? 'No, it wasn't a matter of any forced choice. I didn't take a stand to die or fall by poetry. I simply turned from one thing to another'" (Cook, *A Living Voice*, p. 12).

8. That there is perceptibly a link between "The Wood-Pile" and "The Tuft of Flowers" is suggested as well by Poirier, *Work of Knowing*, p. 143.

9. "Directive," p. 521.

10. *Walden*, pp. 250-51.

11. "Elegiac Stanzas," in *The Poetical Works of Wordsworth*, ed. Thomas Hutchinson, revised by Ernest de Selincourt (London: Oxford Univ. Press, 1950), pp. 452-53.

12. Mertins, *Life and Talks—Walking*, p. 76.

13. *Letters of Frost to Untermeyer*, p. 37.

14. Cook, *A Living Voice*, p. 50.

15. Thompson, *Early Years*, p. 553. For accounts of the fire at Derry, see Thompson, *Early Years*, p. 301, and *New Hampshire's Child: The Derry Journals of Leslie Frost*, notes and index by Lawrance Thompson and Arnold Grade (Albany: State Univ. of New York Press, 1969), book 1, pp. 26 and 31.

16. *Selected Letters of Robert Frost*, p. 220.

17. *Collected Works of Emerson*, vol. 1: *Nature, Addresses, and Lectures*, introduced by Robert E. Spiller, text established by Alfred R. Ferguson (Cambridge, Mass.: Harvard Univ. Press, 1971), p. 10. With Emerson's notation of "perfect exhilaration" while crossing the "bare common, in snow puddles," compare lines from Frost's poem, "Clear and Colder—Boston Common": "As I went down through the common, / Then felt I first delight / Of the city's thronging winter days / And dazzling winter night" (*Robert Frost: Poetry and Prose*, p. 199).

18. *Walden*, p. 67.

19. *Nature*, p. 14.

20. "The Bonfire," in *Complete Poems, 1949*, p. 165.

21. "Fire and Ice," in *Complete Poems, 1949*, p. 268.

22. *Walden*, p. 254. It is possible that besides encountering this

statement in *Walden,* Frost also knew its source in Thoreau's journals. See Michael West, "Versifying Thoreau: Frost's 'The Quest of the Purpled Fringed' and 'Fire and Ice,'" *English Language Notes* 16 [September 1978]:44-47).

23. "Beyond Words," in *Complete Poems, 1949,* p. 556.

24. *Walden,* pp. 304-9.

25. "A Hillside Thaw," in *Complete Poems, 1949,* pp. 293-94.

8. ECONOMY

1. Mertins, *Life and Talks—Walking,* p. 210.

2. Denis Donoghue, *Connoisseurs of Chaos: Ideas of Order in Modern American Poetry* (New York: Macmillan, 1965), pp. 182-84.

3. Malcolm Cowley, "Frost: A Dissenting Opinion," *New Republic,* September 11, 1944, pp. 312-13; "The Case against Mr. Frost: II," September 18, 1944, 345-47. His strictures on "Two Tramps in Mud Time" appear on pp. 345-46.

4. See, for example, Frost's poem "To a Thinker" (originally entitled "To a Thinker in Office"); *Interviews with Robert Frost,* pp. 82-88; *Letters of Frost to Untermeyer,* pp. 251, 258-59, 268, 280, 345; *Selected Letters of Robert Frost,* pp. 413-15, 430, 442-43, 450, 493-94.

5. "Two Tramps in Mud Time," in *Complete Poems, 1949,* pp. 357-59.

6. *Walden,* p. 251.

7. In 1934 the ninth line of the poem read: "Good blocks of *beech* it was I split" (emphasis added). Through several reprintings the line remained unchanged—until *Complete Poems* in 1949, when for the first time the word "oak" replaces "beech." As originally published, however, lines 9-12 (quoted in the text) bear some resemblance to an observation in Thoreau's journals. In 1858 Thoreau wrote: "Minott remembers how he used to chop beech wood. He says that when frozen it is hard and brittle just like glass, and you must look out for the chips, for, if they strike you in the face, they will cut like a knife" (*The Writings of Henry David Thoreau,* 17 [Boston: Houghton Mifflin, 1906]: 250). As early as 1896 Frost was acquainted with excerpts from Thoreau's journals (Thompson, *Early Years,* p. 218). In the context of Thoreau's warning that in chopping one must be wary of *beech* chips that "cut like a knife," it can be seen just how emphatically Frost celebrates his own skill at splitting beech wood: "every piece I squarely hit / Fell splinterless as a cloven rock." It can be noted further that, although the time is April, the incident reported in Frost's poem occurs when "Winter was only playing possum," with "lurking frost in the earth beneath / That will steal forth after the sun is set / And show on the water its crystal teeth"—at a time, in short, when beech wood still has the properties it acquires only when "frozen." One can only speculate on the reason for the change from "beech" to "oak" fifteen years after the poem was first published. One possibility is that by 1949

Frost's distance from the Thoreauvian influences on his poem enabled him to revise the poem along purely euphonic lines.

8. *Writings*, 4:458.

9. Ibid., p. 459.

10. Ibid., p. 468.

11. Ibid., p. 461.

12. Ibid. For correctives to the 1930s view of Thoreau as a collectivist thinker, see Heinz Eulau, "Wayside Challenger: Some Remarks on the Politics of Henry David Thoreau," *Antioch Review* 9 (1949): 509-22; Leo Stoller, *After Walden: Thoreau's Changing Views on Economic Man* (Stanford: Stanford Univ. Press, 1957), particularly the last two chapters; and Sherman Paul, *The Shores of America: Thoreau's Inward Exploration* (Urbana: Univ. of Illinois Press, 1958), p. 251 and passim.

13. Interview in *Rural America* (June 1931), reprinted in *Interviews with Robert Frost*, pp. 77-78.

14. *Writings*, 4:477.

15. Ibid., 7:300.

16. Interview in the *Boston Post Magazine* (April 27, 1952), reprinted in *Interviews with Robert Frost*, p. 133.

9. SMOKE

1. *Walden*, p. 253.

2. "Snow," in *Complete Poems, 1949*, p. 185.

3. *Walden*, p. 252.

4. "The Cocoon," in *Complete Poems, 1949*, p. 310.

5. "Smoke in Winter," in *Collected Poems of Henry Thoreau*, enlarged edition, ed. Carl Bode (Baltimore, Md.: Johns Hopkins Press, 1964), p. 13.

6. Ibid., p. 3.

7. Compare the closing lines of "The World-Soul":

> Spring still makes spring in the mind
>   When sixty years are told;
> Love wakes anew this throbbing heart,
>   And we are never old;
> Over the winter glaciers
>   I see the summer glow,
> And through the wild-piled snow-drift
>   The warm rosebuds below.

(The Complete Poetical Works of Ralph Waldo Emerson [Boston: Houghton Mifflin, 1910], p. 19.)

8. "Storm Fear," in *Complete Poems, 1949*, p. 13.

9. Untitled, in *In the Clearing*, p. 101.

10. *Walden*, p. 323.

11. "A Cabin in the Clearing," in *In the Clearing*, pp. 16-18.

12. "The Figure a Poem Makes," p. v.

10. SOLITARY SINGER

1. "The Oven Bird," in *Complete Poems, 1949*, p. 150.
2. "Dust of Snow," in *Complete Poems, 1949*, p. 270.
3. Laurence Perrine, "Frost's 'Dust of Snow,'" *Explicator* 29 (March 1971), item 61.
4. "My Butterfly," p. 1429.
5. C.G. Jung, *Memories, Dreams, Reflections*, recorded and edited by Aniela Jaffé, trans. by Richard Winston and Clara Winston (New York: Vintage Books, 1965), pp. 39-40.
6. "Dust in the Eyes," in *Complete Poems, 1949*, p. 341.
7. *Selected Letters of Robert Frost*, p. 208.
8. Quoted in Sergeant, *Trial by Existence*, p. 188.
9. Ibid.
10. *Walden*, p. 192.
11. *Journal*, vols. 2, 10, 6, and 1 (pp. 9, 411-12, 251, and 145, respectively), ed. Bradford Torrey, in *Writings*, vols. 8, 16, 12, and 7. Another readily available source for the material was *Thoreau's Bird-Lore, Being Notes on New England Birds from the Journal of Henry D. Thoreau*, ed. Francis H. Allen (Boston: Houghton Mifflin, 1910), pp. 356-59.
12. *Journal*, vol. 13 (p. 301), (*Writings*, 19:301).
13. See Bradford Torrey, "Thoreau as a Diarist," *Atlantic Monthly* 95 (January 1905): 16; Walter Harding, *The Days of Henry Thoreau* (New York: Knopf, 1965), p. 297; and *Thoreau on Birds*, ed. Helen Cruickshank, foreword by Roger Tory Peterson (New York: McGraw-Hill, 1964), p. 167.
14. Bradford Torrey, "A Day in the Franconia Mountains," *Independent* 52 (June 14, 1900): 1425.
15. Cruickshank, *Thoreau on Birds*, p. 167.
16. *Interviews with Robert Frost*, p. 174.
17. Mildred Howells, "'And No Birds Sing,'" *Atlantic Monthly* 96 (November 1905): 712. Although I have not come across the external evidence to prove that Frost knew Miss Howells's poem, it would be surprising, particularly given the importance of the *Atlantic Monthly* to any aspiring poet of the day, to learn that he had not seen it. William Dean Howells he knew and admired; see, for example, *Selected Letters of Robert Frost*, pp. 174, 179, 191, 265-66.
18. Quoted in Sidney Hayes Cox, "The Sincerity of Robert Frost," *New Republic*, August 25, 1917, p. 109; and quoted again in Cox, *A Swinger of Birches: A Portrait of Robert Frost* (New York: Collier Books, 1961), p. 21.
19. *Interviews with Robert Frost*, p. 21.

11. SWINGING

1. Cook, *A Living Voice*, p. 232.
2. Jarrell, *Poetry and the Age*, p. 37.

3. Sergeant, *Trial by Existence*, p. 116.

4. *Journal*, vol. 4, in *Writings*, 10:435. All page numbers in my text refer to this edition and volume.

5. "Birches," in *Complete Poems, 1949*, pp. 152-53.

6. *Selected Letters of Robert Frost*, p. 89.

7. The trope is common enough. Recent usages include Erica Jong's novel *Fear of Flying* (1973) and John Updike's collection of reviews and essays *Hugging the Shore* (New York: Vintage, 1984), p. 624.

8. William B. Ober, *Boswell's Clap and Other Essays: Medical Analyses of Literary Men's Afflictions* (Carbondale: Southern Illinois Univ. Press, 1979), p. 34.

9. "Education by Poetry," in *Selected Prose of Robert Frost*, p. 39. Frost's notion that a poet "rides" a metaphor has affinities with William James, who writes: "Any idea upon which we can ride, so to speak; any idea that will carry us prosperously from any one part of our experience to any other part, linking things satisfactorily, working securely, simplifying, saving labor; is true for just so much, true in so far forth, true instrumentally" ("Pragmatism," in *Pragmatism and Other Essays*, p. 28).

10. "The Figure a Poem Makes," p. viii.

11. *Selected Letters of Robert Frost*, pp. 418-19.

12. "Two Tramps in Mud Time," p. 359.

13. Quoted in *The Pocket Book of Robert Frost's Poems*, introduced by Louis Untermeyer, with commentary (New York: Pocket Books, 1946), p. 87.

14. Cook, *A Living Voice*, p. 230.

15. Ibid.

16. Ibid., p. 51.

17. Ibid., p. 114.

18. Quoted by Cook, "Frost in Context," p. 146. Cook continues with his own understanding of what Frost meant by "the renewal of words": "He meant, I inferred, that poetry had to do with the etymological association of words and that in writing, words were twice born when freshly used" (p. 146).

19. "Bond and Free," in *Complete Poems, 1949*, p. 151.

20. *Collected Works of Emerson*, 1: 10.

21. Ibid., p. 31.

22. "Desert Places," in *Complete Poems, 1949*, p. 386.

23. *Prose Jottings of Robert Frost: Selections from His Notebooks and Miscellaneous Manuscripts*, ed. Edward Connery Lathem and Hyde Cox (Lunenburg, Vt.: Northeast—Kingdom, 1982), p. 141.

24. Cook, *A Living Voice*, p. 232.

12. NATURE'S GOLD

1. *Collected Works of Emerson*, 1:17.

2. Ibid., p. 22.

3. "Mowing," in *Complete Poems, 1949*, p. 25.
4. *Collected Works of Emerson*, 1:44.
5. "Pragmatism," in *Pragmatism and Other Essays*, p. 21.
6. *Collected Works of Emerson*, 2:202.
7. "Away!" in *In the Clearing*, p. 15.
8. "Kitty Hawk," in *In the Clearing*, pp. 48-49.
9. "Perfect Day—A Day of Prowess," in *Selected Prose of Robert Frost*, p. 87.
10. *Collected Works of Emerson*, 2:198.
11. "After Apple-Picking," in *Complete Poems, 1949*, pp. 88-89.
12. *Walden*, p. 71.
13. Ibid., p. 5.
14. Ibid., p. 6.
15. Ibid., p. 238.
16. "Unharvested," in *Complete Poems, 1949*, p. 400.
17. *Walden*, p. 166.
18. Ibid., pp. 310-11.
19. "Nothing Gold Can Stay," in *Complete Poems, 1949*, p. 272.
20. "Hyla Brook," in *Complete Poems, 1949*, p. 149.

13. LINKED ANALOGIES

1. *A Boy's Will* (London: David Nutt, 1913), p. ix. These glosses disappeared in all subsequent printings of the poem. All further quotations from "The Tuft of Flowers" come from *Complete Poems, 1949*, pp. 31-32.
2. *North of Boston* (London: David Nutt, 1914), p. x. This gloss was also dropped in reprintings of the poem. All subsequent quotations from "Mending Wall" come from *Complete Poems, 1949*, pp. 47-48.
3. Two exceptions, both of which acknowledge Frost's link but do almost nothing with the clue, are Elizabeth Shepley Sergeant, *Fire under the Andes: A Group of North American Portraits* (New York: Knopf, 1927), pp. 296-97; and John Robert Doyle, Jr., *The Poetry of Robert Frost: An Analysis* (Johannesburg: Witwatersrand, 1962), pp. 208-9.
4. Quoted in Sergeant, *Trial by Existence*, p. 67. It is of interest that Frost credited a public reading of this poem in 1906 with his being hired to teach at Pinkerton Academy; see Thompson, *Early Years*, pp. 318-23.
5. See Waggoner, *American Poets*, pp. 307-8. The Emerson texts he finds significant are an essay and a poem, both entitled "Friendship."
6. *Collected Works of Emerson*, 2:184.
7. Ibid.
8. Ibid., pp. 184-85.
9. Ibid., 1:28.
10. *Letters of Frost to Untermeyer*, p. 10.
11. *Selected Letters of Robert Frost*, p. 344.

12. See *Refranes y frases proverbiales Españolas de la edad media*, compiled by Eleanor S. O'Kane, Anejos del Boletín de la Real Academia Española, 2 (Madrid: Academia Española, 1959): 182; *12.600 refranes más*, compiled by Francisco Rodríguez Marín (Madrid: Tipografía de la "Revista de Archivos, Bibliotecas y Museos," 1930), p. 249; and R. Foulché-Delbosc, "Proverbes judéo-espagnols," *Revue hispanique* 2 (1895): 350. In the United States the proverb appears, exactly as Frost gives it, in *Blum's Farmer's and Planter's Almanac* (Winston-Salem, N.C.: John Christian Blum, 1850), p. 13; see Addison Barker, "Good Fences Make Good Neighbors," *Journal of American Folklore* 64 (1951): 421.

13. *The Journals and Miscellaneous Notebooks of Ralph Waldo Emerson*, ed. Ralph H. Orth, vol. 6: *1824-1838* (Cambridge, Mass.: Harvard Univ. Press, 1966): 161. Orth cites Knox's *Elegant Extracts* as Emerson's source.

14. *Journals of Ralph Waldo Emerson*, ed. Edward Waldo Emerson and Waldo Emerson Forbes (Boston: Houghton Mifflin, 1910), 4:238.

15. See John C. Messenger, Jr., "The Role of Proverbs in a Nigerian Judicial System," *Southwestern Journal of Anthropology* 15 (Spring 1959): 64-73, and Kwesi Yankah, "Proverb Rhetoric and African Judicial Processes: *The Untold Story*," *Journal of American Folklore* 99 (July-September 1986): 280-303.

16. *Journal* (11:338), in *Writings*, vol. 17.

17. Compare Emerson, who writes in "Intellect": "God offers to every mind its choice between truth and repose. . . . He in whom the love of repose predominates, will accept the first creed, the first philosophy, the first political party he meets,—most likely his father's. . . . He in whom the love of truth predominates, will keep himself aloof from all moorings and afloat. He will abstain from dogmatism, and recognize all the opposite negations between which, as walls, his being is swung" (*Collected Works of Emerson*, 2:202). In "Quotation and Originality" Emerson put it simply: "The child quotes his father, and the man quotes his friend" (*Complete Works of Emerson*, 8:190). Consequently, in "Mending Wall," the neighbor quotes his father and the speaker quotes his neighbor.

18. Edith Hamilton, *Mythology* (New York: New American Library, 1953), p. 44.

19. Oskar Seyffert, *A Dictionary of Classical Antiquities*, revised and edited by Henry Nettleship and J.E. Sandys (New York: Meridian Library, 1956), p. 621.

20. *Walden*, p. 249.

14. DOMINION

1. *Selected Letters of Robert Frost*, p. 426.
2. *Collected Works of Emerson*, 1:19.

3. "The White-Tailed Hornet," in *Complete Poems, 1949*, pp. 360-62.

4. "Pragmatism," in *Pragmatism and Other Essays*, pp. 131-32.

5. "The Comic," in *Complete Works of Emerson*, 8: 158.

6. Quoted in Nitchie, *Human Values*, p. 158.

7. J. Henri Fabre, *The Hunting Wasps*, translated by Alexander Teixeira de Mattos (New York: Dodd, Mead, 1915), p. 138. For the matter of Frost's general interest in Fabre (and Henri Bergson), see Lawrance Thompson, *Robert Frost: The Years of Triumph, 1915-1938* (New York: Holt, Rinehart and Winston, 1970), p. 300. Elizabeth Shepley Sergeant, who would later write extensively about Frost's life and poems, published an essay, "The Real Fabre," in *New Republic*, February 6, 1915, pp. 25-26. She comments at one point: "In short, Fabre can see no point of fusion between instinct and reason; and it is interesting that Bergson quotes these studies of paralyzing wasps in a 'Creative Evolution' to confute the neo-Darwinians and support his distinction between reason and intuition." It is likely that Frost knew this essay, for in the same issue the *New Republic* published his poem "The Death of the Hired Man" (pp. 19-20).

8. Fabre, *Hunting Wasps*, p. 138.

9. Ibid., p. 16.

10. Ibid., p. 37.

11. Fabre had said of the wasps: "Their eyes and their memory possess a sureness that is very nearly infallible" (ibid., p. 331).

12. Ibid., p. 54.

13. "The Literate Farmer and the Planet Venus," in *Complete Poems, 1949*, pp. 509-13.

14. *Letters of Frost to Untermeyer*, p. 47. See, in particular, Fabre's chapter on the insect's instinctive faculties accompanied by its inability to reason, "The Ignorance of Instinct" (*Hunting Wasps*, pp. 188-211), which begins:

> The Sphex has shown us how infallibly and with what transcendental art she acts when guided by the unconscious inspiration of her instinct; she is now going to show us how poor she is in resource, how limited in intelligence, how illogical even, in circumstances outside of her regular routine. By a strange inconsistency, characteristic of the instinctive faculties, profound wisdom is accompanied by an ignorance no less profound. To instinct nothing is impossible, however great the difficulty may be. In building her hexagonal cells, with their floors consisting of three lozenges, the Bee solves with absolute precision the arduous problem of how to achieve the maximum result at a minimum cost, a problem whose solution by man would demand a powerful mathematical mind. The Wasps whose larvae live on prey display in their murderous art methods hardly rivalled by those of a man versed in the intricacies of anatomy and physiology. Nothing is difficult to instinct, so long as the act is not outside the unvarying cycle of

animal existence; on the other hand, nothing is easy to instinct, if the act is at all removed from the course usually pursued. The insect which astounds us, which terrifies us with its extraordinary intelligence surprises us, the next moment, with its stupidity, when confronted with some simple fact that happens to lie outside its ordinary practice.
15. "Not All There," in *Complete Poems, 1949*, p. 408.
16. "The Comic," p. 159.
17. Untitled, in *In the Clearing*, p. 39.
18. "The Comic," p. 164.
19. Ibid., p. 169.
20. "Pragmatism," in *Pragmatism and Other Essays*, p. 131.
21. "The Demiurge's Laugh," in *Complete Poems, 1949*, p. 35.

15. SUBSTANTIATION

1. "On Emerson," in *Selected Prose of Robert Frost*, p. 111.
2. Ibid.
3. Ibid., p. 114.
4. "The Pasture," in *Complete Poems, 1949*, p. 1.
5. "Kitty Hawk," in *In the Clearing*, p. 7.
6. *Collected Works of Emerson*, 1:22.
7. *Selected Prose of Robert Frost*, p. 118. See also Cook ("Frost in Context"), who on two occasions quotes Frost: "'That's what the Christian religion means—God's own descent into flesh meant as a demonstration that the supreme merit lay in risking spirit in substantiation" (p. 173); and "It's an adventure of the spirit into the material; that's religion" (p. 168).
8. Quoted in Robert F. Fleissner, "'Frost . . . at . . . Play': A Frost-Dickinson Affinity Affirmed," *Research Studies* 46 (March 1978): 38.
9. *Selected Prose of Robert Frost*, pp. 118-19. Compare, as well, these sentences from an interview published in the *New York Times Book Review*, October 21, 1923: "America means certain things to the people who come here. It means the Declaration of Independence, it means Washington, it means Lincoln, it means Emerson—never forget Emerson" ("'We seem to lack the courage to be ourselves,'" in *Interviews with Robert Frost*, p. 50).
10. "Concord Hymn," in *Complete Poetical Works of Emerson*, pp. 158-59.
11. *Selected Prose of Robert Frost*, p. 119.
12. Ibid., p. 115.
13. Quoted in Gorham B. Munson, *Robert Frost: A Study in Sensibility and Good Sense* (New York: Haskell House, 1967), p. 98. Compare Emerson, who in "The Poet" wrote, "Words are also actions, and actions are a kind of words" (*Collected Works of Emerson*, 3:6).
14. *Selected Prose of Robert Frost*, p. 116.

15. "A Soldier," in *Complete Poems, 1949*, p. 332.

16. "The Divinity School Address," in *Collected Works of Emerson*, 1:80, 81.

17. Robert Frost, "Nothing More Gentle than Strength," *New Republic*, April 9, 1962, p. 21.

18. "Poetry and Imagination," in *Complete Works of Emerson*, 8:35.

16. TRIBUTARIES

1. Barry, *Frost on Writing*, pp. 144-48.

2. "Smoke in Winter," p. 13.

3. *Prose Jottings*, p. 78. Elsewhere Frost remarked somewhat moralistically that the poet's task was "to purify words until they meant again what they should mean" (*Robert Frost: Poetry and Prose*, p. 388).

4. "The Pasture," p. 1.

5. "Pertinax," in *Complete Poems, 1949*, p. 407.

6. *A Masque of Reason*, in *Complete Poems, 1949*, p. 598.

7. "Accidentally on Purpose," in *In the Clearing*, p. 34.

8. *Prose Jottings*, p. 48.

9. Ibid., p. 16. Frost continues: "It is like a sapling. Set it out and watch it ramify and proliferate."

10. Ibid., p. 13.

11. Ibid., pp. 46-47.

12. Ibid., p. 11.

13. *A Masque of Reason*, p. 601.

14. "Uriel," in *Complete Poetical Works of Emerson*, p. 14.

15. Quoted in Morrison, "The Agitated Heart," p. 79.

16. "West-Running Brook," in *Complete Poems, 1949*, p. 329.

17. *Prose Jottings*, p. 34.

INDEX

Acts, 124
Adam, 64, 117, 118, 119
Aiken, Conrad, 31
American Academy of Arts and
    Sciences, 138, 140
Amherst College, 9, 24-26, 29, 45, 57
Amherst Student, 107
Amherst Writing, 3
Anderson, Charles R., 64
*Anthology of Magazine Verse for
    1915,* 100
Arnold, Matthew: "Thyrsis," 157 n
    10
*Arts Anthology: Dartmouth Verse,
    1925,* 3
Atlantic Monthly, 70, 79, 100, 164 n
    17

Bartlett, John T., 104
Bergson, Henri, 135, 168 n 7
Bianchi, Martha Dickinson
    (Madame), 9, 27, 28
Bingham, Millicent Todd, 27, 29
Bishop, Elizabeth, 25
Bogan, Louise, 24-25, 26
Boswell, James, 106
Braithwaite, William Stanley, 100
Brault, Gerard J., 159 n 11
Bread Loaf School of English, 25, 99,
    108
British Broadcasting Corp., 58
Brower, Reuben A.: *Robert Frost:
    Constellations of Intention,* 156-57
    n 5
Browne, George, 3, 147, 148
Browne and Nichols School, 3, 4, 147
Browning, Elizabeth Barrett, 25

Bryant, William Cullen, 21; "To a
    Waterfowl," 155 n 10, 157 n 7
Burns, Robert, 19
Burrell, Carl, x
Burroughs, John, 21

Carman, Bliss, 40
"Choice of Two Paths, The," 44, 45,
    50, 51
Christianity, 139, 169 n 7
Ciardi, John, 25
Cole, Charles W., 24, 25, 57
Coleridge, Samuel Taylor, 68, 69
Cook, Reginald L., 25, 29, 57, 58, 99,
    159 n 6, 160-61 n 6, 165 n 18, 169 n
    7; *Robert Frost: A Living Voice,* 99,
    161 n 7
Coverdale, Miles (*Blithedale
    Romance*), 66-67
Cowley, Malcolm, 77, 78, 80, 81
Cox, Hyde, 29
Cox, Sidney, 63, 94
Crane, Stephen: "A man feared that
    he might find an assassin," 53
Crosse, Henry, 45-46

Dana, Mrs. William Starr: *How to
    Know the Wild Flowers,* x, 22
Dante Alighieri: *Inferno,* 40, 44-45,
    46, 50, 51, 53
Dartmouth College, 13, 40, 41, 58
Darwin, Charles, 77, 131, 135
Darwinism, 76-77, 81, 168 n 7
Declaration of Independence, 169 n 9
Dickinson, Emily, x, 6, 9-33, 42, 49,
    57, 138, 150, 155 n 10
—books: *Bolts of Melody,* 29;

Complete Poems of Emily Dickinson, 27, 28, 29; *Poems*, 10, 11, 13, 26, 27, 29; *Poems, Second Series*, 10, 13, 22, 26, 27, 29, 49; *Poems, Third Series*, 19
—poems: "An altered look about the hills," 16; "Apparently with no surprise," 16; "Beauty—be not caused—It is," 29; "Because I could not stop for Death," 27; "A Bird came down the Walk," 27; "The Bustle in the House," 27; "The Clouds their Backs together laid," 10, 31; "From cocoon forth a butterfly" ("The Butterfly's Day"), 14-15, 18; "The gentian weaves her fringes," 21; "God made a little gentian" ("Fringed Gentian"), 21-22; "The Heart asks Pleasure—first," 29; "Heart, we will forget him!" 19; "I Know that he exists," 19-20; "I like to see it lap the miles," 27; "I never saw a Moor," 27; "I reason, earth is short," 11-12; "I stepped from Plank to Plank," 27; "I taste a liquor never brewed," 18, 27; "In Winter in my Room," 27; "The Mountains grow—unnoticed," 10, 30; "My cocoon tightens, colors tease" ("From the Chrysalis"), 16, 17, 27; "My life closed twice before its close," 10, 28, 32; "My Life had stood—a Loaded Gun," 26; "A narrow Fellow in the Grass," 27; "Our journey had advanced," 49-50; "Poor little heart!" 19; "Some things that fly there be," 13; "The Soul selects her own Society," 29; "The Spider as an Artist" ("Cobwebs"), 16-17, 27; "A spider sewed at night" ("The Spider"), 16-17; "Tell all the Truth but tell it slant," 20, 29, 57; "There is a word," 19; "There's a certain Slant of light," 27; "Two butterflies went out at noon" ("Two Voyagers"),

13-14, 18; "A Word made Flesh is seldom," 138
Dickinson celebration (Amherst College, 1959), 9-10, 24-26, 29
Donoghue, Denis, 76-77, 78, 81

Ecclesiastes, 118
Eden, 60-61, 63-65, 117, 121
Edison, Thomas, 135
Eliot, Thomas Stearns: *The Waste Land*, 34, 93
Emerson, Ralph Waldo, ix, x-xi, 2, 6, 21, 31, 34, 57, 63, 71, 72, 77, 115, 117, 124-25, 131, 132-33, 135, 136, 137, 138, 140, 141, 142-43, 147-48, 150, 151, 169 n 9
—books: *Nature*, 71, 109-10, 115, 116, 125, 130, 140, 161 n 17; notebooks and journals, 82, 126
—essays: "Circles," 124-25, 150; "The Comic," 132, 136; "The Divinity School Address," 143, 147; "Forebearance," 123; "Friendship," 166 n 5; "Inspiration," 90; "Intellect," 167 n 17; "On the Relation of Man to the Globe," 34, 157-58 n 15; "The Over-Soul," 2; "The Poet," 115, 169 n 13; "Poetry and Imagination," 143, 157 n 8; "Quotation and Originality," x-xi, 6, 44, 154 n 9, 167 n 17; "Resources," ix; "Uses of Great Men," 76
—poems: "Brahma," 138-39; "The Concord Hymn," 141-42; "Each and All," 155 n 10; "Friendship," 166 n 5; "The Rhodora," 155 n 10; "Uriel," 151; "Woodnotes," 22; "The World-Soul," 85, 163 n 7
Emerson-Thoreau Medal, 138
Emily Dickinson: Three Views, 24
Eve, 64, 117, 118

Fabre, J. Henri, 131, 133-34, 135, 168 nn 7, 11, 168-69 n 14

Fales Library, New York University, 24, 26, 27, 28

Frost, Elinor (White), vii, 18, 26, 28, 155 n 16

Frost, Robert: "Moth and Butterfly" book, 16, 35, 155 n 12; poetry and poetic theories, vii, 1, 3-4, 4-5, 5-6, 10, 20, 30-33, 40, 47, 58, 65, 70, 89, 94, 97, 98, 106-7, 109, 125-26, 141, 142, 147-48, 150, 151, 152, 161 n 7, 165 n 18, 170 nn 3, 9; reading, x-xi, 3, 5-6, 150, 152; schooling and education, x, 59-63, 150, 151
—books: *A Boy's Will*, x, 48, 123; *Complete Poems of Robert Frost, 1949*, xii, 162 n 7; *A Further Range*, 36, 76, 130; *In the Clearing*, xii, 51, 86, 87, 117, 139, 149; *A Masque of Mercy*, 53; *A Masque of Reason*, 91, 149, 150-51; *Mountain Interval*, 32, 45, 94, 109; *New Hampshire*, 50, 90, 159-60 n 12; *North of Boston*, 27, 100, 123, 139; *Prose Jottings*, 110, 147, 148, 149-50, 152, 170 n 9; *Steeple Bush*, 1; *Three Poems*, 155 n 16; *West-Running Brook*, 83, 93, 142
—essays: "Education by Poetry," 106; "The Figure a Poem Makes," 89, 106-7, 160 n 13; "Nothing More Gentle than Strength," 143; "Of Axe-Handles and Guide-Book Poetry," 58, 98, 164 n 19; "On Emerson," 138-42; "The Prerequisites," xi, 5-6; "The Unmade Word, or Fetching and Far-Fetching," 3, 4-5, 147-48
—poems: "Accidentally on Purpose," 149; "After Apple-Picking," 117-20; "All Revelation," 109; "Away!" 117; "The Ax-Helve," 58-65, 70, 159-60 n 12; "Beyond Words," 73; "Birches, 2, 4-5, 91, 99-111; "The Birds do Thus," 11-12; "Blue-Butterfly Day," 15-16; "Bond and Free," 109; "The Bonfire," 70-72; "A Cabin in

the Clearing," 87-88; "Clear and Colder—Boston Common," 161 n 17; "The Cocoon," 83-84; "The Death of the Hired Man," 168 n 7; "The Demiurge's Laugh," 123, 136-37; "Departmental," 130-31; "Desert Places," 109, 110; "Design," 16, 17, 34-43, 149, 156-57 n 5, 157 n 15; "Directive," 1, 2, 151; "The Draft Horse," 51, 52-53;"A Drumlin Woodchuck," 130; "Dust in the Eyes," 90, 93; "Dust of Snow," 90, 91, 92; "The Exposed Nest," 161 n 7; "Fire and Ice," 72-73, 161-62 n 22; "Forgive, O Lord, my little jokes on Thee," 20, 136; "For Once, Then, Something," 2; "A Hillside Thaw," 73-75; "Hyla Brook," 33, 122; "In White," 16, 17, 35-43, 156 n 3; "In winter in the woods alone," 86-87; "Kitty Hawk," 117, 139-40; "The Literate Farmer and the Planet Venus," 131, 134-35; "Mending Wall," 33, 53, 123, 125-29, 166 n 3, 167 n 17; "Mowing," 115, 116; "My Butterfly," 12-13, 15, 16, 17, 40, 41-42, 90, 91, 92, 154-55 n 8; "Not All There," 135; "Nothing Gold Can Stay," 121-22; "On the Heart's Beginning to Cloud the Mind," 130; " 'Out, Out'—," 161 n 7; "The Oven Bird," 90, 93-98, 117, 122; "Pan with Us," 123; "The Pasture," 139, 148-49; "Pertinax," 149; "Pod of the Milkweed," 17-18; "The Quest of the Orchis" ("The Quest of the Purple Fringed"), x, 2, 20-21, 155 n 22, 161-62 n 22; "Revelation," 19, 20; "The Road Not Taken," 44-53; "The Secret Sits," 20; "Snow," 82-83; "A Soldier," 142-43; "A Star in a Stone-Boat," 109; "Stars," 109; "Stopping by Woods on a Snowy Evening," 16, 50-51, 52, 53; "Storm Fear," 85-86; "To a Thinker" ("To a

Thinker in Office"), 162 n 4; "The
Tuft of Flowers," 15, 16, 67-68, 123,
124, 127, 161 n 8, 166 n 2, 166 n 4;
"Two Tramps in Mud Time," 53,
76-81, 108, 130, 162-63 n 7;
"Unharvested," 120; "Warning,"
18-19, 155 n 15, 16; "West-Running
Brook," 151-52; "The White-Tailed
Hornet," 130, 131-35; "The Wood-
Pile," 53, 67-70, 121, 160 n 3,
160-61 n 6, 161 n 8

Garden of Eden, 60-61, 63-65, 117,
121
Garfunkel, Art: "The Dangling
Conversation," 24
Genesis, 64, 119-20, 157 n 8
Gibson, Wilfred, 108
God, 16, 19, 20, 64, 67, 92-93, 103,
117, 129, 135-36, 137, 139, 143, 169
n 7
Green, Charles, 24

Harvard University, 63, 70, 71
Hawthorne, Julian: "Design," 41, 42
Hawthorne, Nathaniel, 69; The
Blithedale Romance, 66, 160 n 3
Hemingway, Ernest, 40
Holmes, Oliver Wendell: "The
Chambered Nautilus," 34
Hovey, Richard: "Seaweed," 40, 41,
157 n 10
Howells, Mildred, 95; " 'And No
Birds Sing,' " 97-98, 164 n 17
Howells, William Dean, 95, 164 n 17

Independent 11, 12, 20, 22, 25, 40,
41, 42, 154-55 n 8, 155 n 15, 157 n
10

James, William, x, 6, 42;
"Pragmatism," 136, 157-58 n 15,
165 n 9; "Pragmatism and
Religion," 131-32; "Will to
Believe," 49, 116, 132
Jarrell, Randall, 100; Poetry and the
Age, 156-57 n 5

Jefferson, Thomas, 141
Jesus, 143
Job, 91-92, 149
Johnson, Thomas H.: Emily
Dickinson: An Interpretive
Biography, 28
Jones Library (Amherst), 9, 24, 25
Jong, Erica, 106
Jung, Carl, 92-93

Keats, John, 5, 97; "Ode to a
Nightingale," 31-32; "On First
Looking into Chapman's Homer,"
31-32
Kemp, John, x
Knox, Vicesimus: Elegant Extracts,
126, 167 n 13

Lathem, Edward Connery, xii
Lawrence (Mass.) High School, ix,
10, 26
Lincoln, Abraham, 141, 169 n 9
Longfellow, Henry Wadsworth, x, 6,
40, 49; Inferno (translation), 44-45,
50, 51, 53; "My Lost Youth," 48;
"Seaweed," 155 n 10
Lowell, Robert, 25
Lydgate, John: Reson and
Sensuallyte, 44

MacLeish, Archibald, 24, 26; J.B., 25
Maeterlinck, Maurice, 133
Mark (Saint), 1
Marlowe, Christopher: "Come with
me and be my love," 149
Meiklejohn, Alexander, 45
Melville, Herman: Moby-Dick, 35;
"The Whiteness of the Whale," 35
Mertins, Louis, 29; Robert Frost: Life
and Talks-Walking, 24-25
Middlebury College: Abernethy
Collection, 6
Milton, John: "Lycidas," 157 n 10
Morris, Lewis: "From an American
Sermon," 42
Moses, 103
Mother Goose, 29, 31

nature, ix-x, 4, 44, 58, 60-65, 67, 69, 72, 76-77, 86-87, 95-96, 101-4, 109-10, 111, 115, 117, 119, 121-22, 125, 130-32, 135-36, 141
Neo-Darwinians, 168 n 7
New Deal, 77
New Republic, 77
New York University: Fales Library, 24, 26, 27, 28
Nietzsche, Friedrich: *Also Sprach Zarathustra,* 99
Norton, Charles Eliot: *Inferno* (translation), 46, 50

Palgrave, Sir Francis: *Golden Treasury,* 40
parable, 1, 2, 4, 57, 97
Parsons, Thomas William: *Inferno* (translation), 40
Pater, Walter, 71-72
Pentecost, 124
Perrine, Laurence, 90-91
Pocket Book of Robert Frost's Poems, 99-100
Poe, Edgar Allan, 40
Poetry and the Age, 156-57 n 5
Poirier, Richard, 157-58 n 15, 161 n 8
Pope, Alexander, 130
Power, Sister Mary James: *In the Name of the Bee,* 28
proverbs, 126-27, 129, 167 n 12
Psalms, 67, 131-32

Rand, Frank Prentice: *The Jones Library in Amherst,* 9
Roosevelt, Franklin Delano, 77

Sappho, 9, 25
Saturday Review of Literature, 29
Sedgwick, Ellery, 70
Sergeant, Elizabeth Shepley, 40, 48, 57, 94, 100, 168 n 7; *Robert Frost: The Trial by Existence,* 40-41, 46-47
Shakespeare, William, 60, 96, 139; *Hamlet,* vii
Shapiro, Karl, 25

Shelley, Percy Bysshe: "Adonais," 5, 157 n 10
Simon, Paul: "The Dangling Conversation," 24
Social Darwinism, 76-77, 81
Stephen, Fitz-James, 49
Swift, Jonathan, 130

Taggard, Genevieve: *The Life and Mind of Emily Dickinson,* 28, 29
Terminalia, 129
Terminus, 129
Therien, Alek, 159 n 11
Thermopylae, 142
Thomas, Edward, 46, 47-48
Thompson, Lawrance, x, 10-11, 13, 18, 48, 58, 70, 155 n 16, 157 nn 7, 15
Thoreau, Henry David, 2, 6, 21, 30-31, 57-65, 66, 67, 68, 69, 71, 73, 74, 75, 77, 78-81, 82-88, 95, 96, 98, 100-104, 108, 116, 119, 120-21, 122, 128, 129, 138, 148, 149, 150, 159 nn 7, 11, 161-62 n 22, 162-63 n 7, 163 n 12
—books: *Journals,* 100-104, 128, 159 n 11, 161-62 n 22, 162-63 n 7; *Walden,* x, 1, 2, 4, 34, 57-65, 66, 71, 73-74, 79, 82, 83, 87, 95, 119-20, 121, 129, 130, 150, 159 n 11, 161-62 n 22
—essay: "Life without Principle," 79-81
—poems: "Smoke," 83; "Smoke in Winter," 84-85, 148, 149; "Within the circuit of this plodding life" ("Winter Memories"), 85, 86
Todd, Mabel Loomis, 26, 27, 28
Torrey, Bradford, 95, 96-97
Turgenieff, Ivan, 58

Untermeyer, Louis, 28, 70
Updike, John, 106

Viereck, Peter, 25
Vulcan, 129

Waggoner, Hyatt: *American Poets,* 166 n 5

Walden Pond, 2, 82, 95, 149
Ward, Susan Hayes, 35, 40, 41, 43,
   46, 154-55 n 8
Ward, William Hayes, 25, 40
Washington, George, 141, 169 n 9
Washington Monument, 141
Whicher, George F.: *Emily
   Dickinson,* 28; *This Was a Poet,* 28
White, Elinor. *See* Frost, Elinor
   White

Whitman, Walt, 93; "Crossing
   Brooklyn Ferry," 125
Wilbur, Richard, 5, 6, 24, 25, 26;
   "Poetry's Debt to Poetry," 1
Wordsworth, William, 68, 69;
   "Elegiac Stanzas," 69; "Lines
   Composed a Few Miles above
   Tintern Abbey," 85